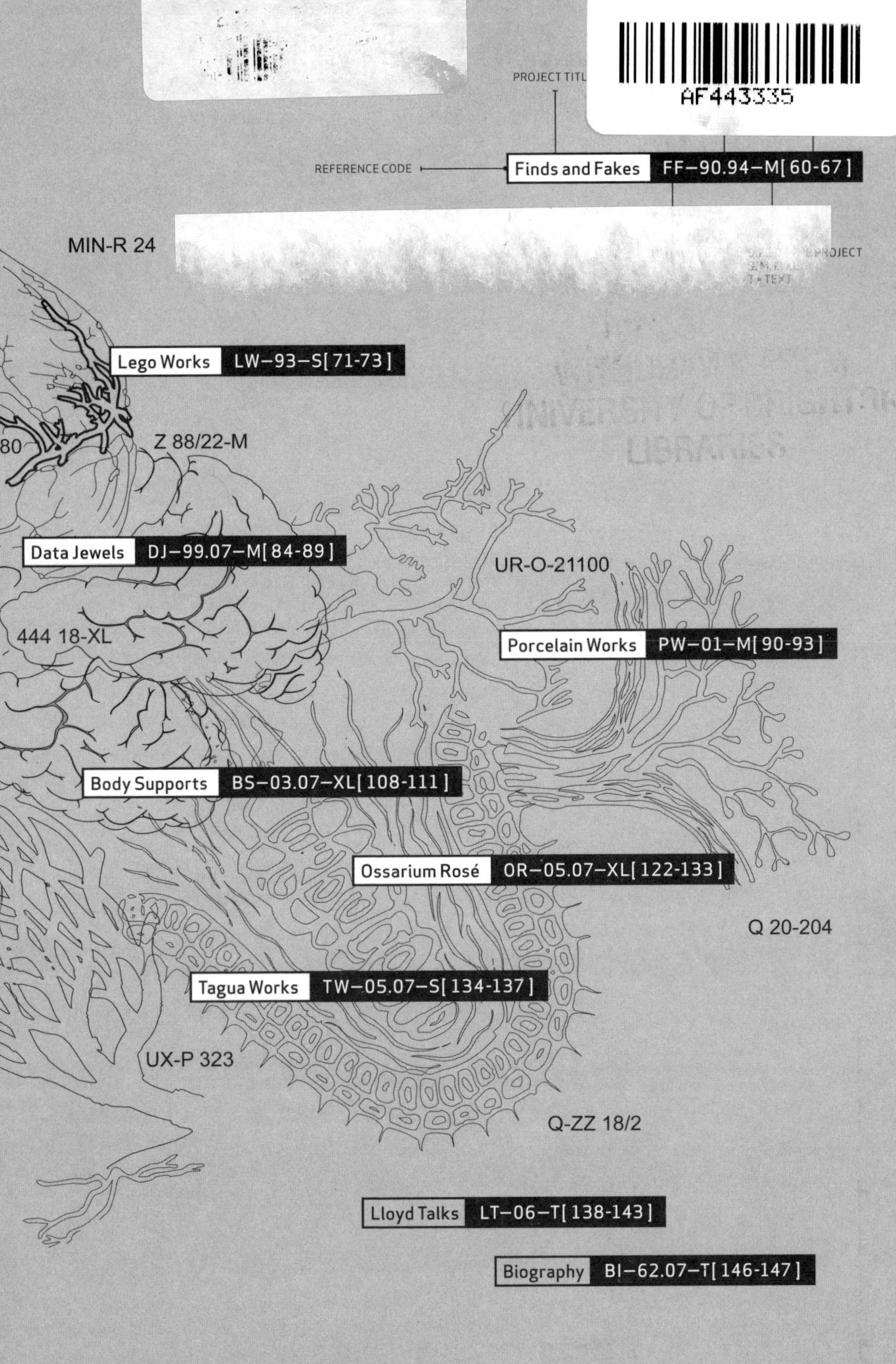

AF443335
PROJECT TITLE
REFERENCE CODE
Finds and Fakes   FF—90.94—M[60-67]
MIN-R 24
Lego Works   LW—93—S[71-73]
Z 88/22-M
8 80
Data Jewels   DJ—99.07—M[84-89]
UR-O-21100
444 18-XL
Porcelain Works   PW—01—M[90-93]
Body Supports   BS—03.07—XL[108-111]
Ossarium Rosé   OR—05.07—XL[122-133]
Q 20-204
Tagua Works   TW—05.07—S[134-137]
UX-P 323
Q-ZZ 18/2
Lloyd Talks   LT—06—T[138-143]
Biography   BI—62.07—T[146-147]

[PW-0]

Christoph Zellweger chooses to make jewellery for many reasons, but its relationship with the body, in an era when our bodies are contested sites, is a driving force. He undertakes an intensive search to understand the way we fit into the world and how we want to shape it. His thoughts have always embraced philosophy, politics and science, genetics and ethics, nature and artifice. This jeweller recognises that the shape of our future existence lies in the delicate interrelationship between nature and technology and while scientists and technologists are responsible for progressing this, artists can reflect, commentate and dispute.

Zellweger's career has a deep root, which gives his work special authority. Whilst most contemporary jewellers are art-school trained with little early background experience, Zellweger's family members have been goldsmiths, silversmiths and watchmakers forsix generations. He has thus been immersed in the world of preciousness and refinement from the day he was born, setting up in him the paradox of the secure rebel. This is a vital clue to the character of his oeuvre: while his *Body Pieces* and other objects to wear exude virtuosity in their craftsmanship and functionality, they eschew conventional forms and materials and insistently question the cultural and social status quo. His jewellery, arresting in its own right, is nevertheless a means to an end. Through it, Zellweger asks questions beyond aesthetics, wearability and function: "What is it in our lives that has real value? What defines value today?"

This spirit of enquiry started early. After leaving school and following on from a work placement, he started a formal goldsmith's apprenticeship with the master craftsman Wilhelm Reindl in Lubeck, on the northern coast of Germany. There, Zellweger was hardworking, good at making, a success. The diligence and skill he showed during these years created a firm foundation to his career, taking him from Lubeck to Geneva and Lenzburg in Switzerland, where he worked as a fine-jeweller, model-maker and designer, finally as head of a leading jewellery workshop for production in Zurich.

During almost a decade in the trade in the 1980s, he knew that life is not only about achievement. He was interested in politics and was part of the environmental movement at the time. He was critical, but not through his work. Feeling trapped in the confines of theestablished jewellery trade with its single-minded focus oncraftsmanship, Zellweger finally left his job, with the conviction that life is not just about making beautifully refined and expensive things, but also about expression, about making a difference.

Christoph's Laboratory

Martina Margetts

Senior Tutor, Critical & Historical Studies. Royal College of Art, London

[PW–0] Seeds, 2001. Porcelain, leather

Christoph's Laboratory

Christoph Zellweger macht aus unterschied-
lichen Gründen Schmuck. Es ist aber der
Bezug zum Körper, speziell in einer Zeit in
der dieser zum hart umkämpften Terrain
geworden ist, der ihn antreibt. Er betreibt
intensive Studien, um zu verstehen, wie wir
in diese Welt passen und wie wir sie formen
wollen. Schon immer hat sein Denken Philo-
sophie, Politik und Naturwissenschaft,
Genetik und Ethik, Natur und Künstlichkeit
mit einbezogen. Diesem Schmuckmacher ist
bewusst, dass die Gestalt unserer zukünf-
tigen Existenz im zerbrechlichen Zusammen-
spiel von Natur und Technologie liegt, und
während Wissenschaftler und Technologen
dafür verantwortlich sind, die Welt voran-
zutreiben, reflektieren, kommentieren und
disputieren die Künstler diese wechselvolle
Beziehung.

Zellweger hat eine lange berufliche Entwicklung hinter sich, was seiner Arbeit besondere
Autorität verleiht. Während die meisten
zeitgenössischen Schmuckmacher auf einer
Kunsthochschule ausgebildet wurden und
über wenig Praxiserfahrung verfügen, gibt es
in Zellwegers Familie Gold-, Silberschmiede
und Uhrenmacher seit sechs Generationen.
Er wurde in eine Welt der Präziosen und der
Präzision hineingetaucht, was ihn paradoxer-
weise auch zum Rebellen werden liess. Dies
ist ein vitaler Schlüssel zum Verständnis
seines Werks; während seine *body pieces* und
andere Objekte getragen werden, strahlen
sie virtuose Machart und Funktionalität aus;
genauso meiden sie aber konventionelle
Formen und Materialien und hinterfragen
den kulturellen und gesellschaftlichen Status

quo. Sein Schmuck, auf seine ganz eigene Art
atemberaubend, ist nur Mittel zum Zweck.
Durch ihn stellt Zellweger Fragen, die über
Ästhetik, Tragbarkeit und Funktion hinaus-
gehen: „Was in unserem Leben ist wirklich
von Wert? Wie definieren sich Werte heute?"
Dieser Forscherdrang äußerte sich früh.
Nach der Schulzeit begann er eine Ausbil-
dung zum Goldschmied beim Handwerks-
meister Wilhelm Reindl in Lübeck, an der
norddeutschen Ostseeküste. Dort arbeitete
Zellweger hart und kam voran – er hatte
Erfolg. Die Ausdauer und die handwerk-
lichen Fähigkeiten, die er in diesen Jahren
entwickelte, bildeten eine solide Grundlage
für eine Karriere, die ihn von Lübeck nach
Genf und Lenzburg in die Schweiz führte,
wo er als Juwelen-Goldschmied, Modellma-
cher und Designer arbeitete; schließlich als
Chef d'Atelier in der Produktion bei einem
führenden Schmuckhersteller in Zürich.
In den 1980er Jahren, nach fast einem Jahr-
zehnt im Metier, wusste er, dass das Leben
nicht nur aus Erfolg besteht. Er war interessiert an Politik und Teil der damaligen
Umweltbewegung. Er war kritisch – aber
nicht in seiner Arbeit. Er fühlte sich als
Gefangener des etablierten Schmuckhandels
mit seinem einseitigen Fokus aufs formale
Handwerk. Zellweger verliess schliess-
lich seine Stelle in der Überzeugung, dass
das Leben nicht nur darin besteht, schön
geschaffene und teure Dinge herzustellen,
sondern auch darin sich auszudrücken, um
einen Unterschied zu machen.

Zellweger war angetrieben seiner Arbeit
einen Sinn zu geben. Am *Royal College of
Art* in London fand er die intellektuell stimu-
lierende Umgebung und den interdiszipli-

[FB-0]

Drawn by the urge to give meaning to his work, the Royal College of Art in London provided the environment for intellectual stimuli and interdisciplinary discourse. He found kindred spirits, such as the artists Emma Woffenden and Naomi Filmer, who were also examining the body as conceptual arena. In the 1990s Zellweger, an experienced maker, had the advantage that he could realise any idea he toyed with, any viewpoint he wished to materialise. Like a well-trained athlete, he raised the bar with every piece, every process, from working medical steel - "a nightmare" - to the obsessive enterprise of moulding expanding polystyrene (*Commodity Chains*) or flocking bones (*Ossarium Rosé*).

The impassioned discourse which Zellweger articulated in his jewellery rests on fundamentals: "the excitement of discovery" (a biography of Thomas Edison was a first love) and the wish to determine the point of existence: "I am interested in reality." Reality is of course a moving target (hence his interest in Jean Baudrillard's definition of the hyperreal), encompassing the life on the street and the life of the mind, the beautiful and pleasurable, the abject and mundane, the superficial, consumerist world of products and appearances, and the intangible, ineffable inner world of emotion and belief. Fate may have made Zellweger a jeweller but he is a philosopher in disguise.

Choosing to express his feelings, views and values through jewellery, Zellweger has consistently sought to create wearable objects to define what he calls the object-landscape in a technologically fast advancing culture. The series of rusted steel brooches from 1993/94, for example – with no name because they refer to something we don't know – emulate nature's organic structures and processes, as if Zellweger is "unearthing the future". Each brooch is at once vulnerable and perplexing, beautiful and strong. They are speculative objects: "if you hold a piece in your hands, you start to contemplate what the future could be about," he says. These intriguing works justify their existence by offering a corrective to the possible future we are making for ourselves.

The metamorphosis, corruption even, of nature towards artifice is an enduring issue for this artist. If plant and animal hybrids, clones even, can seem 'natural', Zellweger's view is that the human body will be, is already, the next arena for assault. "The body becomes an artefact, a luxury product", he says, "because it becomes a matter of design". The two monumental *Chains* from 1995, in the British Crafts Council's national collection, eloquently fuse Zellweger's concerns about nature and the body, the natural and the synthetic. These engulfing chains are three to four metres long and made of rusted as well as highly polished surgical steel,

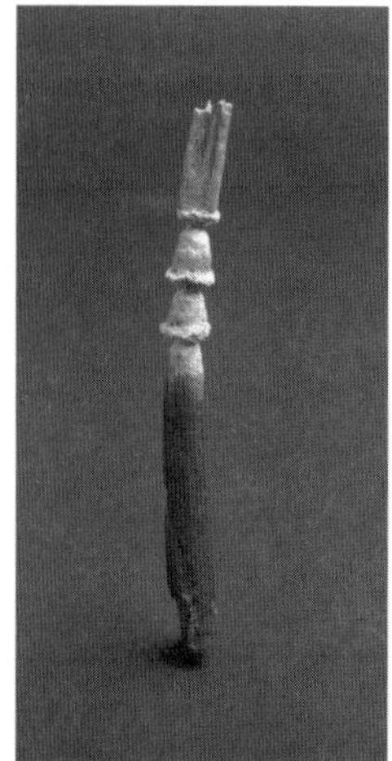

Brooch, 1991.
Wooden-stick.
Pattern created with
teeth

Ring and tool, 1992. Iron, wood, 22ct gold.
Form follows reason

[FB-0] Foreign Bodies #0008530 and #0008740, 2003. Medical stainless steel, bone. Private Collection

nären Diskurs den er gesucht hatte. Er traf
auf Gleichgesinnte, wie die Künstlerinnen
Emma Woffenden und Naomi Filmer, die
ebenfalls den Körper als konzeptuelle Arena
erforschten. In 1990er Jahren hatte Zellweger, damals bereits ein erfahrener Designer, den Vorteil, dass er jede Idee, mit der er
spielte, jeden Blickwinkel, den er zu verwirk-
lichen suchte, auch realisieren konnte.
Wie ein gut trainierter Athlet erhöhte er
die Messlatte mit jedem Stück, mit jedem
Prozess, von der Verarbeitung von medizinischem Stahl – „ein Alptraum" – , bis zum
verrückten Unterfangen, Styropor selbst
aufzuschäumen (*Warenketten*) oder Knochen
mit Flock zu überziehen (*Ossarium Rosé*).
Der leidenschaftliche Diskurs, den Zellweger
über seinen Schmuck ausdrückt, hat seine
Fundamente in der „Lust am Entdecken"
(eine Biographie von Thomas Edison war
eine erste Liebe) und im Wunsch, den Sinn
unserer Existenz mitzubestimmen: „Ich bin
an der Wirklichkeit interessiert." Realität ist
natürlich, ein bewegliches Ziel (daher sein
Interesse an Jean Baudrillards Definition
der Hyperrealität) und umfasst das Leben
auf der Strasse und im Geist, das schöne und
angenehme, das gewöhnliche und oberflächliche, es umfasst die konsumierbare Welt
der Produkte und Bildeindrücke wie auch die
unfassbare, unbeschreibliche innere Welt der
Gefühle und Überzeugungen. Wohl hat das
Schicksal Zellweger zu einem Schmuckmacher gemacht, in Wirklichkeit aber ist er ein
Philosoph – ein unerkannter.
Entschlossen seine Gefühle, Ansichten und
Werte in Form von Schmuck auszudrücken,
strebt Zellweger konsequent danach trag-
bare Objekte zu kreieren, die er als Objekt-

landschaften in einer technologisch schnell
voranschreitenden Kultur umschreibt. Die
Serie verrosteter Broschen von 1993/94 zum
Beispiel - ohne Namen, denn sie beziehen sich
auf etwas, das wir nicht kennen – emulieren
die organischen Strukturen und Prozesse
der Natur, als beabsichtige Zellweger, "die
Zukunft auszugraben". Jede Brosche wirkt
sowohl verletzlich wie verwirrend, schön und
stark. Es sind spekulative Objekte: „Wenn
du ein Stück in den Händen hältst, fragst du
danach, wie die Zukunft aussehen könnte",
sagt er. Diese faszinierend-irritierenden
Arbeiten rechtfertigen ihre Existenz, in
dem sie ein Korrektiv zur möglichen Zukunft
anbieten, die wir für uns machen.
Die Verwandlung, gar Zersetzung der Natur
in Richtung Künstlichkeit ist ein stetig
wiederkehrendes Thema für diesen Künstler.
Wenn Pflanzen- und Tierkreuzungen,
selbst Klone, als „natürlich" angesehen
werden, so wird oder ist für Zellweger der
menschliche Körper die nächste Arena,
die gestürmt wird. „Der Körper wird zum
Artefakt, zu einem Luxusprodukt", sagt er,
„da er zum Gegenstand von Design wird".
Die zwei monumentalen *Ketten* von 1995
(sie befinden sich in der nationalen Samm-
lung des *British Craft's Council*) verbinden
gekonnt Zellwegers Auseinandersetzung
mit Natur und Körper, dem Natürlichen
und dem Synthetischen. Diese verschlun-
genen Ketten sind drei bis vier Meter lang
und aus verrosteten wie auch polierten,
medizinischen Stahlelementen gefertigt,
die mit Latexschläuchen verbunden sind.
Diese Ketten sind Schlüsselwerke in der
Entwicklung von Zellwegers ästhetischem
Vokabular. Er stellt die Frage, ob der mensch-

[FF–0] Ring, 1999. Stainless steel, ceramic shell casting

Fibrecan
ENGLAND
PD12
F 70 SP
STYLE-PLUS

interconnected with latex tubing. The chains are key transitional works in the development of Zellweger's aesthetic vocabulary. He poses the question if the human body in its current way of functioning and in its appearance is appropriate to suit people's expectations and rising demands. Considering the possibilities of genetic engineering, cosmetic and transplant surgery and the synthetic experiences offered by virtual reality, the driving human impulse to experiment, to innovate and to apparently perfect, leads Zellweger to give a negative answer.

This artist is wary of a human drive for perfectability, professionally, emotionally, sexually. He juxtaposes this with an attention to the imperfection and vulnerability of being human. An extended series of polystyrene brooches from 1996/97, fragile Body Pieces, have the appearance of a part of the body, a nodule, a gland, a part of a limb, or they could be pills or synthetic implants. They underline the see-saw ethics and aesthetics of the natural and artificial, the organic and the manipulated in a consumerist world. For Zellweger expandable polystyrene serves as metaphor; it is a white, lightweight and omnipresent material, which one normally associates with disposable packaging. Its cell-like structure is not dissimilar to the architecture of organic matter, although it is artificially produced. The symbiosis between high and low culture, between art and the everyday, complexifies the relationship and purposes of commercial and cultural production.

What has made Zellweger's work – jewellery, products, objects, installations and occasional performances –both topical and poignant for over fifteen years is its embodiment of these concerns.He asks us to confront the problematic juxtapositions of the base and the sublime, the lies and truths in advertising and daily experience, but also the importance of rituals, that delineate the human condition. Zellweger cleverly exposes the ambiguities of our contemporary behaviour and values through the ambiguities of imagery and material in his work. One moment he borrows material from the internet or the world of consumer toys, such as *Tamagotchi* and *Lego*, the next imagery from "untouched nature", eroded rocks and bleached animal bones. Lego, rocks, bones, expanded polystyrene – they are all about commenting on the way we do things. They also act as "relics" of our time.

Zellweger recognises the attraction of the interactive virtual *Tamagotchi* toy, which required its owner to care for its everyday needs, and internet games and services, all

Tamagotchi-pendant, 1992. Silver

[FF–00] Cup, 1999. Stainless steel, ceramic shell casting

liche Körper in seiner Funktionsweise und
in seiner Erscheinung tauglich ist, um den
Erwartungen und steigenden Ansprüchen der
Menschen weiterhin zu genügen. Zellweger
kommt zu einer negativen Antwort, denn er
zieht in seine Betrachtungsweise die sich
auftuenden Möglichkeiten der Gentechno-
logie, der kosmetischen Chirurgie sowie der
Transplantationsmedizin mit ein. Auch ist
er überzeugt, dass die synthetischen Erfahrungen, die durch virtuelle Realitäten beeinflusst werden, das menschliche Denken, das
geleitet ist durch den menschlichen Impuls zu
experimentieren, zu erfinden und zu perfek-
tionieren, verändern.

Dieser Künstler begegnet dem menschlichen
Streben nach Perfektion mit Misstrauen,
beruflich, gefühlsmässig, sexuell. Er stellt
die Unvollkommenheit und Verletzlichkeit
Mensch zu sein dagegen. Eine aufwen-
dige Serie von Broschen aus Styropor von
1996/97, fragile *Body Pieces*, erscheinen
wie Teile eines Körpers: Drüsen, Knöt-
chen, Körperglieder. Sie könnten aber auch
Pillen oder künstliche Implantate sein. Sie
unterstreichen die schnelllebige Ethik und
Ästhetik des Natürlich-Künstlichen und
Biologisch-Manipulierten in einer auf den
Konsumenten ausgerichteten Welt. Für
Zellweger ist Styropor auch als Metapher
zu verstehen; es ist ein weisses, leichtge-
wichtiges, allgegenwärtiges Material, das
für gewöhnlich mit Wegwerf-Verpackungen
assoziiert wird. Sein zellartiger Aufbau ist
der Struktur organisch-körperlichem Materials nicht unähnlich, obwohl es künstlich
produziert wird. In der Symbiose zwischen
hoher- und populärer Kultur, zwischen Kunst
und Alltag zeigt sich die Vielschichtigkeit

und die Absicht kommerzieller und kultu-
reller Produktion.

Diese zielgerichtete Verkörperung seiner
Themen hat Zellwegers Werk – Schmuck,
Produkte, Objekte, Installationen und gele-
gentliche Performances – seit über fünf-
zehn Jahren zugleich aktuell und prägnant
gemacht. Er fordert dazu auf, sich mit
dem problematischen Nebeneinander von
Sublimem und Profanem, mit den Lügen und
Wahrheiten in der Werbung und den alltäglichen Erfahrungen wie auch mit der Wichtigkeit der Rituale, die die menschliche Existenz
umreissen, näher zu befassen. Raffiniert
entblößt Zellweger Doppeldeutigkeiten
unserer heutigen Verhaltensweisen und
Werte, in dem sein Werk durch die geschickte
Wahl von Bildern und Material Mehrdeutig-
keiten evoziert. Einmal borgt er sich Material
aus dem Internet oder der Spielzeug-Waren-
welt, wie beispielsweise mit *Tamagotchi*
und *Lego*, ein andermal mit Bildern „unbe-
rührter Natur", wie erodierten Steinen und
gebleichten Tierknochen. Lego, Knochen,
Steine, Styropor – sie sind alle Kommentare
zu dem, wie wir etwas tun. Sie agieren als
„Reliquien" unserer Zeit.

Zellweger anerkennt die Attraktivität des
virtuellen, interaktiven *Tamagotchi* Spiel-
zeugs, das von seinem Besitzer fordert,
es täglich zu pflegen, und die Internet
Spiele und Dienstleistungen, die die einmal
gemeinsam gelebten Rituale und Erfahrungen aus Religion und Familie ersetzen.
Doch erforscht er dieses Terrain aus einer
gesellschaftskritischen Warte.

Zellweger bedient mit seiner Arbeit keine
konventionelle Ästhetik. „Das ist für mich
keine formale Übung", betont er. Er verführt

[RH-0]

[RH-00]

of which he feels provide the rituals once offered by shared experiences of religion and family, but he also explores this territory as a warning, as social critique.

Zellweger does not supply conventional beauty in his work. "It's not a formal exercise," he says. He tries to seduce through surface texture and form. But behind his seduction is uncertainty. There is the importance of touch - but repulsion - is a constant theme. His chains, pins, bones are important to handle: they become humanised as wearable. The meaning is shifted by shifting the context. He is loading the object with association, trying to define what jewellery can be.

With the *Rhizome* series, Zellweger reveals the importance of ornament and pattern, the essence of how structure of thought becomes visible. It is pattern with purpose: like sea ripples because of the current, a roof pattern which helps stop the rain or an arabesque because of belief. The computer offers a tool for dealing with complexity and for both spontaneity and control. When Zellweger does "push to the minimum", he uses the appropriate materials and technology to make his points: waterjet and lasers to produce intimate works to touch in warm and flexible natural rubber, or highly polished medical steel to make a point about precision and clinical coldness.

"I love to be in between the traditional categories, art and design," Zellweger says. For him it is not about 'fitting in', but about making work to move people. There are parallels between his concerns and those of artists like Stelarc, Daniele Buetti, the Chapman brothers or some Droog designers. Thinking about ways of living, human relationships, beauty and death, and getting involved emotionally in exploring the body as object, are common ground. From his readings of Paul Virilio, Hans Jonas and Michael Foucault, he is aware of the metamorphosis of real time and space, the simulation of reality and the complex ambiguities of living in our bodies.

Zellweger's extensive career, with exhibitions in the museums and galleries of eighteen countries, has also profoundly embracededucation, in Britain, Europe and the United States. This has been important for both Zellweger and his students, providing an opportunity to test ideologies and identities and questions of value. Teaching allows him to be "a sparring partner" for his students: through his feedback, his handling of structures, his aesthetics and propositions, his students are energised by the exemplar of his purpose and his method. With his concept-led work, Zellweger resonantly explores his purpose: to reflect our time, projecting into the future. **MM**

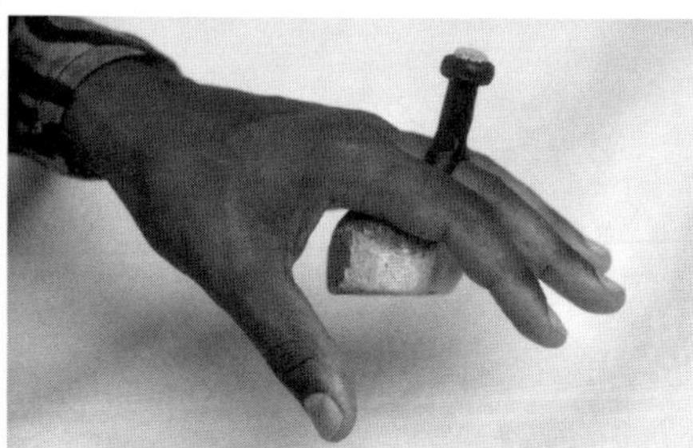

Ring, 1992. Bone, iron, gold. Royal College of Art Collection, London

[RH-00] Project **Material & Technology**, 2002. Haute École d'Arts Appliqués, Geneva

durch Oberflächentextur und Form. Doch
hinter seiner Verführung steht auch Unge-
wißheit. Berühren und gleichzeitig abstossen
sind ständig wiederkehrende Themen. Es ist
wichtig, seine Ketten, Nadeln und Knochen zu
berühren: erst durch das Tragen erhalten sie
eine menschliche Dimension. Die Bedeutung
wird verschoben durch das Verschieben des
Kontexts. Er lädt das Objekt mit Assoziationen auf und definiert auf diese Weise, was
Schmuck sein kann.

Mit der Serie *Rhizome* enthüllt Zellweger die
Wichtigkeit von Ornament und Muster, die
essenziell sind und Strukturen des Denkens
sichtbar werden lassen. Es sind Muster, die
einen Zweck erfüllen: wie Meereswellen,
verursacht durch den Strom, ein Dachmuster,
das hilft den Regen zu stoppen oder eine
Arabeske, die durch den Glauben entsteht.
Der Computer bietet sich als Werkzeug an,
um mit Komplexität, mit Spontaneität und
Kontrolle umzugehen. Zellweger sucht die
Reduktion, er nutzt die entsprechenden
Materialien und Techniken, um seine Ideen
auf den Punkt zu bringen: Wasserstrahl
und Laser, um warm und vertraut wirkende
Arbeiten aus geschmeidigem Naturgummi
herzustellen, oder auf Hochglanz polierten
medizinischem Edelstahl, um über Präzision
und klinische Kälte zu reden.

„Ich mag es, mich zwischen den traditionellen
Kategorien Kunst und Design zu bewegen",
sagt Zellweger. Ihm geht es nicht darum "sich
einzufügen", sondern um Arbeiten zu machen,
die die Leute bewegen. Es gibt Parallelen
zwischen seinen Anliegen und jenen von
Künstlern wie Stelarc, Daniele Buetti,
den Chapman Brüdern oder einigen Droog
Designern. Nachdenken über menschliche
Beziehungen, Schönheit und Tod, darüber
wie man lebt; sich auf die Erforschung des
Körpers als Objekt gefühlsmässig einlassen,
sind Gemeinsamkeiten. Dank der Lektüre von
Paul Virilio, Hans Jonas und Michel Foucault
weiß er um die Verwandlung von Zeit und
Raum, der Simulation von Realität und der
komplexen Zwiespältigkeit, in unseren
Körpern zu leben.

Zellwegers beruflich vielseitige Laufbahn
mit Ausstellungen in Museen und Galerien in
achtzehn Ländern umfasst auch eine intensive Lehrtätigkeit an Design- und Kunsthoch-
schulen vor allem in Grossbritannien, aber
auch in Europa und den Vereinigten Staaten.
Für Zellweger und seine StudentInnen ist es
wichtig, persönliche Wertefragen, Vorstel-
lungen und Identitäten zu testen. Als Dozent
ist Zellweger „Sparring Partner": sein Feedback, seine Art Strukturen anzugehen, seine
Ästhetik und seine Vorschläge treiben seine
Studenten und Studentinnen an, er fordert
und fördert sie, exemplarisch auch durch
seine Zielstrebigkeit, seine Methoden. Zellwegers konzeptuell breit abgestütztes Werk
schafft Resonanz und erreicht sein Ziel: In
dem er unsere Zeit reflektiert, nimmt er die
Zukunft voraus.

Martina Margetts
Dozentin, Critical & Historical Studies,
Royal College of Art, London

[BP-0]

Approach 1

We see: three-dimensional forms, amorphous. Organic, alien flowing? [1]
Or technological with imprints, coding? [2]
Strips, straps. [3]
We compare the forms with ones known, their size with ourselves, our body. [4]
We register colour... [5-6]
Material: metal, leather or texture.
We construe possibilities of use, classification... [7-8]
We admit we are perplexed.
We feel warmth or coldness, color distanced or sugary. [9-10]
Metal as repellent? [11]
Leather as protection or fetter
Texture downy? [12]
– The dawning of one's own experiences –
We think, we guess, we ask – the "object" emerges as provocation.

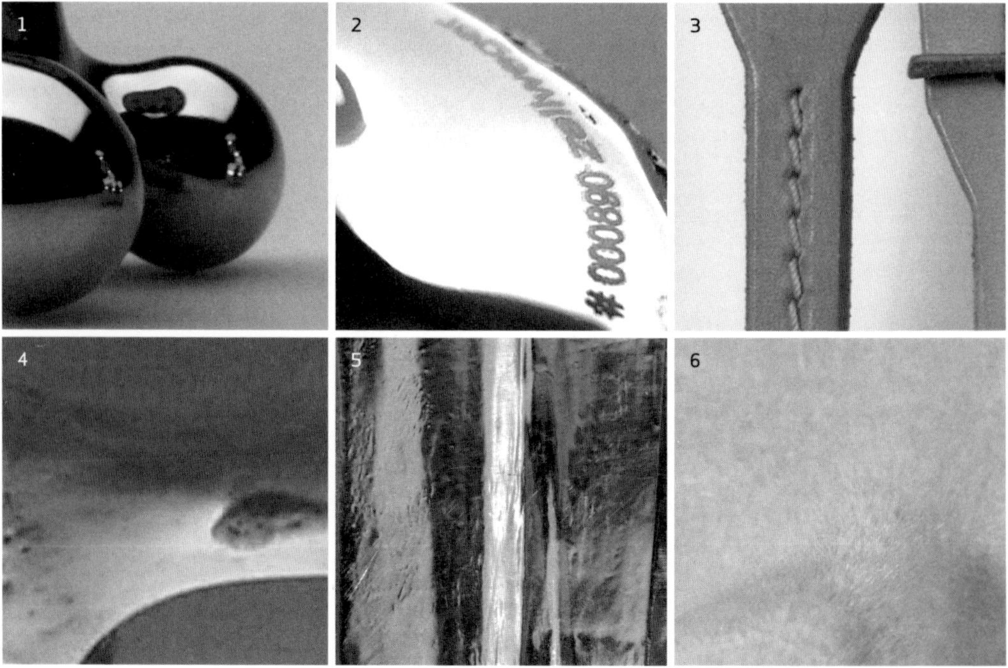

SR–T[22-39]

About the relevance of the seen
A mental wandering of the eye
Dr. Phil. Sabine Runde

Vice Director and Curator of Applied Art 20th + 21st century. Museum of Applied Art Frankfurt

[BP–0] Body Pieces GNY, 1997-1998. Expanded polystyrene, velcro

Zur Relevanz der Bildlichkeit
Eine gedankliche Augenwanderung

Annäherung 1

Wir sehen: dreidimensionale Formen, amorph.
Organisches, fremdartig fließend? [1]

Oder Technisches mit Prägungen, Codierungen? [2]

Streifen, Riemen. [3]

Wir vergleichen die Formen mit Bekanntem,
ihre Größe mit uns, unserem Körper. [4]

Wir registrieren Farbe … [5-6]

Material: Metall, Leder oder Textur.

Wir konstruieren Möglichkeiten der Anwendung, der Einordnung … [7-8]

Wir konstatieren Ratlosigkeit.

Wir empfinden Wärme oder Kälte, die Farbe
distanziert oder süßlich [9-10]

das Metall als abweisend ? [11]

das Leder als Protektion oder Fessel
die Textur flauschig? [12]

– eigene Erfahrungen scheinen auf –

Wir denken, wir rätseln, wir fragen – der
„Gegenstand" entpuppt sich als Provokation.

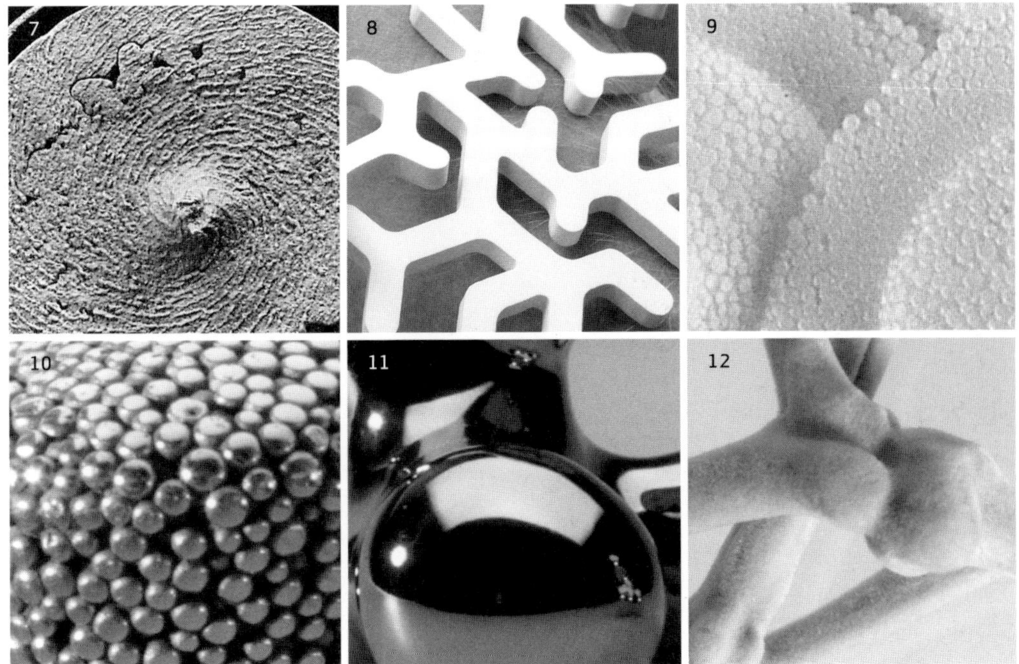

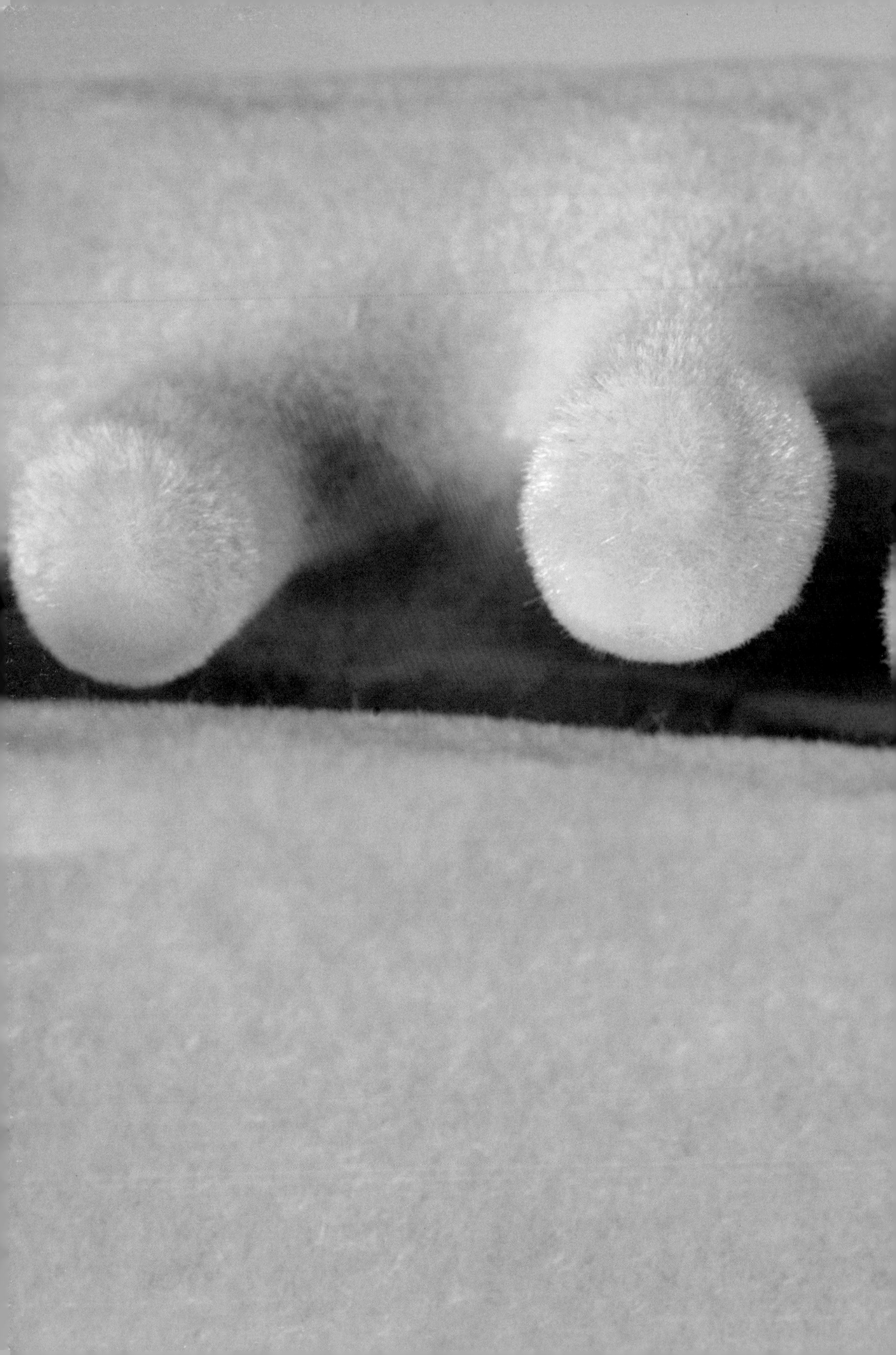

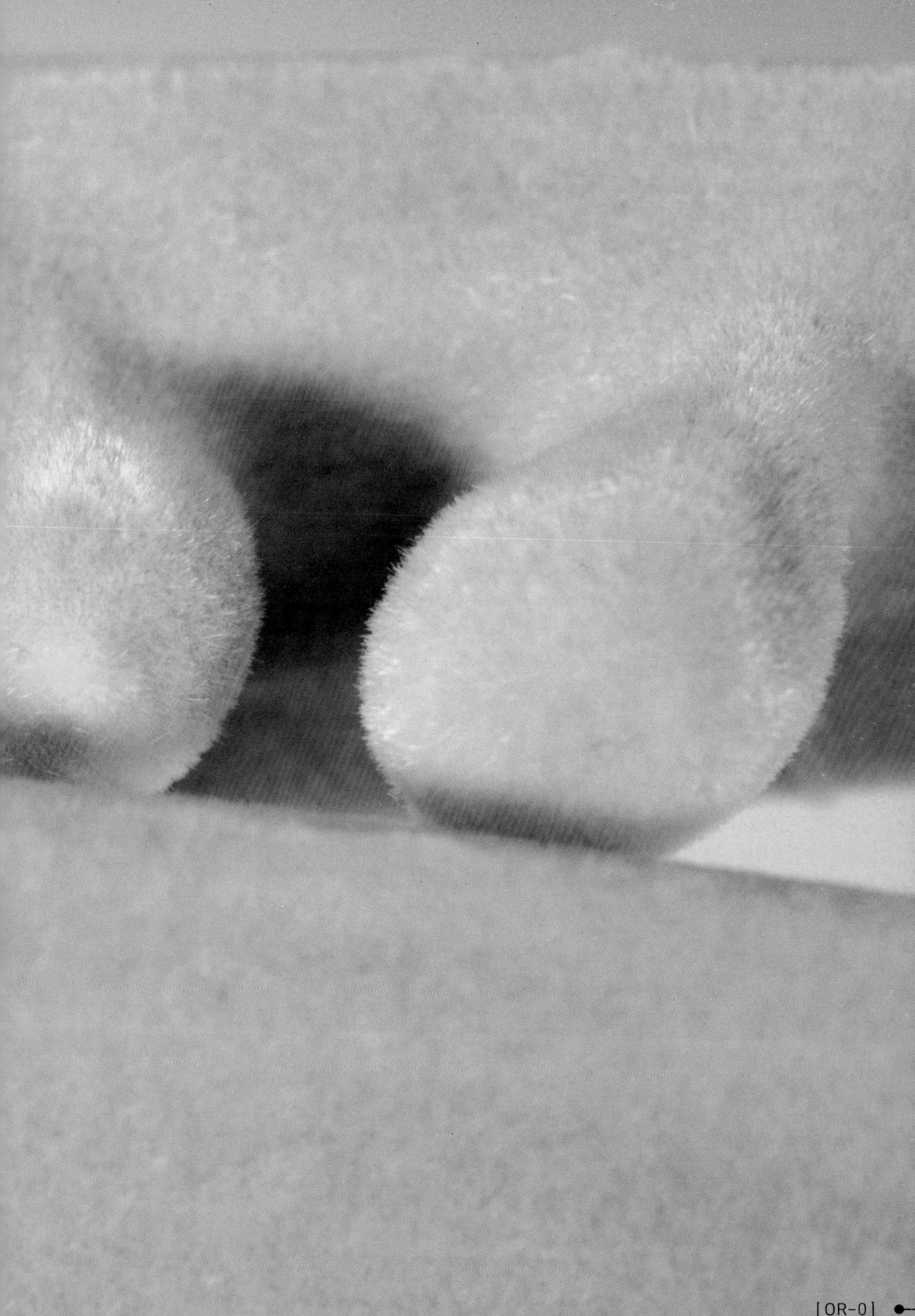

[OR-0]

Approach 2. Discourse

While meeting this challenge, let's take time for a small excursion. First of all we will envision the course of perception. Considered physiologically, as a whole the sequence of discerning and feeling (so-called *perceptio* or the act of perceiving) is a complex, scientifically explainable process. This imparts a sense of reliability and clarity to perception, just as scientific progress enables us to increasingly believe in the explainability of the world. However, let's pay special attention to the following conditions: through the brain and sense organs, the human body is organically pre-determined to feel, smell, hear and see. The sequence of steps or course of detecting, recognizing, comparing and evaluating are nonetheless a necessary prerequisite to attain the stage of mentally processing the perceived (so-called *apperception*). The special capabilities of processing the perceived – considered sociologically – have to be developed; humans develop smelling and hearing before seeing; and, "primary seeing", for example, first begins with simply distinguishing between light and dark.

In fact, the wonder of [modern] medicine itself is not sufficient to operatively produce the physiological prerequisites of seeing, i.e., it is not capable of making the blind see. Rather "seeing" has to be learned from the ground up. The time that we use for this [learning] begins at birth, [a potential which] is finely developed in childhood and then further extended during the rest of our lives. As part of our investigation, let's envision that seeing, recognizing and evaluating are processes of learning. How we recognize, categorize and evaluate the *seen* or viewed is an expression of the respective complex, cultural conditioning of our lives in our times.

Reconstructing the course of seeing, the multileveled sequence of recognizing forms, proportions, materials, we remember the process of learning significations or names, recalling the categorization, definition of meanings and considering the mental processing of the interpreted. Thereby, a broad spectrum of relevant parameters stretches out before us. With the help of these basic points of reference, we determine what we see. Here memory and experience represent [two] elementary vertices.[Both functions are fundamentally characterized by cultural and individual conditioning.]

Annäherung 2. Diskurs

Wie begegnen wir dieser Herausforderung
– nehmen wir uns Zeit für einen kleinen
Exkurs. Vergegenwärtigen wir uns zunächst
den Ablauf der Wahrnehmung. Physiologisch
gesehen ist die Gesamtheit der Vorgänge des
Wahrnehmens und Empfindens (sog. Perzep-
tion) ein komplexer naturwissenschaftlich
erklärbarer Prozess. Das vermittelt Verbind-
lichkeit und Eindeutigkeit der Wahrnehmung,
wie überhaupt der Fortschritt der Naturwis-
senschaften uns die Erklärbarkeit der Welt
immer glaubhafter werden lässt. Schenken
wir jedoch folgenden Umständen besondere
Aufmerksamkeit: Der menschliche Körper
besitzt mit dem Gehirn und den Sinnesor-
ganen die organischen Vorrausetzungen, zu
fühlen, zu riechen, zu hören und zu sehen.
Die Vorgänge des Auffassens, Erkennens,
Vergleichens und Beurteilens sind jedoch
notwendige Voraussetzung, um zu einer
gedanklichen Verarbeitung des Wahrgenommenen (sog. Apperzeption) zu gelangen. Die
besonderen Fähigkeiten, Wahrgenommenes
zu verarbeiten, müssen – sozialisatorisch
betrachtet – entwickelt werden; Riechen und
Hören entwickelt der Mensch vor dem Sehen
und „Primäres Sehen" beispielsweise beginnt
zunächst mit der simplen Unterscheidung
von Hell und Dunkel.

Tatsächlich genügen selbst die Möglichkeiten der Medizin, die physiologische
Vorraussetzung zum Sehen operativ herzustellen, nicht, um einen blinden Menschen
sehend zu machen. „Sehen" muss von Grund
auf gelernt werden. Die Zeit, die wir darauf
verwenden, beginnt mit der Geburt, wird
komplex ausgebildet in der Kindheit und ein
ganzes Leben fortentwickelt. Vergegenwärtigen wir uns für unsere Betrachtungen:
Sehen, Erkennen und Bewerten sind Lern-
prozesse. Wie wir Gesehenes erkennen,
einordnen und bewerten ist Ausdruck der
jeweiligen komplexen kulturellen Prägungen
unseres Lebens in unserer Zeit.

Rekonstruieren wir den Vorgang des Sehens,
den vielschichtigen Ablauf des Erkennens
von Formen, Proportionen, Materialien, erin-
nern wir uns an den Prozess des Erlernens
von Bezeichnungen, vergegenwärtigen uns
das Zuordnen, Definieren von Bedeutungen
und bedenken wir die gedankliche Verarbeitung des Aufgefassten, so fächert sich ein
weites Spektrum relevanter Bezugsgrößen
vor uns auf, mit deren Hilfe wir das, was wir
sehen, bestimmen. Elementare Eckpunkte
stellen darin Erinnerung und Erfahrung
dar. Beide Funktionen sind grundlegend
durch kulturelle und individuelle Prägungen
charakterisiert.

Interim 1

Thinking determines perception – viewed in this way, observation, recognition or even more so, the comprehensive perception of things in the sense of the mental processing of the perceived (*cognition*) can never be the same for any two humans. On the contrary, cognition is not only different individually, but also subjected to the constant change of history.

Co-determined by epochal, cultural and individual change, simplification strategies as the foundations of communication of comparability have served since time immemorial as a self-evident basis of human communication, pragmatically sorted according to so-called "reality-relevant" aspects. Today alone this is required by the flood of visual impressions which are constantly being extended by a growing supply of always newer, always more exciting, but also always more schematic or abstract computer-generated visualities. Our abilities adapt to this everyday phenomenon, i.e., quickly and according to practiced principles to register everything perceived and to categorize the world reduced to coding. The routine of evaluation with all its qualities of differentiation is an automatic procedure, a checklist. To see becomes something unconscious.

Like everything unconscious, a schematized reception is achieved at the expense of experienced or lived space. On the search for a way to balance this loss, we encounter the potential of art. Artistic forms of expression are setting our world in perspective through the absence of rules as canonic form. Seemingly unintentional, its gestalt prohibits a rapid correlation or classification. The forms elude a simplifying tendency. Paradoxically the language of art leads us on mental detours, away from the straight and narrow. The form doesn't adhere to any rule conveying itself rather as an expression of freedom, freedom of perception, freedom of interpretation. Contradictions in perception, ambiguous appearances incite curiosity and make demands upon the energy of the viewer to overcome their apparent reserve to decipher the inconsequential.

Art as elixir and counterweight to organized everyday life fortunately excludes no aspect of life. It cannot be stopped by categorical terms, like "eating", "drinking", "dancing", "adorning oneself".On the contrary, here we can time and again encounter patterns of our own thinking. The mental detour going around our expectations to one of these terms enables us to encounter our own pre-conceptions to this cue. Following this track there is much to be discovered about personal standards and conditioning. Let's end the excursion here with the observation that the scope available for expanding perception can also be developed by exploring our expectations.

[FB– 00] Foreign Bodies, 2002. Medical stainless steel. Worn between fingers

Interim 1

Das Denken bestimmt die Wahrnehmung - so
gesehen, kann Betrachtung, Erkennung oder
besser die umfassende Wahrnehmung der
Dinge im Sinne der gedankliche Verarbeitung
des Wahrgenommenen (der Kognition) unter
den Menschen nicht gleich sein. Im Gegenteil, die Kognition ist nicht nur individuelle
verschieden sondern zudem dem stetigen
Wandel der Geschichte unterworfen.

Vom epochalen, kulturellen und individuellen
Wandel mitbestimmte Vereinfachungs-
strategien als Kommunikationsgrundlage
der Vergleichbarkeit sind seit je her eine
selbstverständliche Grundlage der menschlichen Kommunikation, pragmatisch sortiert
nach sog. ‚realitätsrelevanten' Aspekten.
Das fordert heute allein die Flut an visu-
ellen Eindrücken, die durch ein wachsendes
Angebot immer neuer, reizvoller, aber
schematisierter Computer generierter
Visualitäten ständig erweitert wird. Im
Alltäglichen passen sich unsere Fähigkeiten
an, das heißt, schnell und nach einstudierten
Prinzipien alles Wahrgenommene registrieren und die Welt verkürzt als Codierung
einordnen. Die Auswertungsroutine ist bei
aller Differenziertheit ein automatisierter
Vorgang, ein Abhaken. Sehen wird zu etwas
Unbewusstem.

Eine schematisierte Rezeption geht wie alles
Unbewusste auf Kosten des Erlebnisraums.
Auf der Suche diesen Verlust auszugleichen,
treffen wir auf das Potential der Kunst.

Künstlerische Ausdrucksformen setzen
sich durch Regellosigkeit zur Regelhaftig-
keit unserer Welt in Beziehung. Scheinbar
absichtslos verhindert ihre Gestalt eine
schnelle Zuordnung oder Einordnung. Die
Formen entziehen sich einer vereinfa-
chenden Aneignung. Kontradiktisch führt
uns die Sprache der Kunst auf gedankliche
Um- und Abwege. Die Form hält sich an keine
Regel, vermittelt sich als Ausdruck der Freiheit, Freiheit der Wahrnehmung, Freiheit
der Deutung. Widersprüche in der Wahrnehmung, uneindeutige Erscheinungen erzeugen
Neugier und fordern die Energie des
Betrachters, ihre vordergründige Verschlos-
senheit zu überwinden, Inkonsequenzen zu
enträtseln.

Kunst als Elixier und Gegenpol zum organi-
sierten Alltag schließt erfreulicherweise
keinen Aspekt des Lebens aus. Sie lässt sich
nicht aufhalten von einem kategorischen
Begriffen, wie „Essen" „Trinken" „Tanzen",
„Schmücken", im Gegenteil wir können
hier immer wieder Schablonen unseres
Denkens begegnen. Der gedankliche Umweg
über unsere Erwartungen zu einem dieser
Begriffe lässt uns eigenen Vor- Einstellungen
zu diesem Stichwort begegnen. Auf diesem
Weg ist viel über persönliche Maßstäbe und
Prägungen herauszufinden. Beenden wir den
Exkurs an dieser Stelle mit der Feststel-
lung, dass auch durch Untersuchung unserer
Erwartungen der Freiraum für Wahrnehmung
entwickelt werden kann.

Approach 3

Let's allow ourselves to be led by the refusal of the inspected "objects", which don't permit themselves to be handled in the usual way. Curious about unexpected spaces of thinking, we deepen our first perceptions and extend our point of view via correlations, characteristics, valuations: the metal – not warm gold, but also not silver – actually grey, smooth, cold, mirroring.

We discover: it's about medical steel. Steel – we become conscious of its proverbial precision. Medically – content-related connotations emerge: antiseptic, clinical, technical, cool, existential. Our own recalled experiences accompany the expression that is relevant for us. Do we feel unusually affected by the expressive space of the material?

We ask ourselves: did something comparably irritating already lie in the form? Or did a need/ curiosity prevail upon us to move, to touch the form between the fingers, and playfully experience more about the "thing" and one's own hand? To search for analogies to one's own body, to find its place under the skin?

We discover: material and form in their reciprocal relations.

Interim 2

When exact seeing and reading appear to be only a rational process, then the perception of forms, materials and the relations of phenomena between themselves proceeds obviously less in predetermined calculable ways. These are sensually felt references to what has been seen, experienced, they create spaces of thinking for our associations.

What does the material leather make us think of? Uncolored natural leather. Here we are also invited to remember, do we associate it with braces, orthopedic paraphernalia, orthoses, supporting devices for the musculoskeletal system? Or: a dog leash, a school satchel, sports equipment, a weapon? Once again a strong emotional component is produced through the interaction of form and material, which through our everyday routine is even more difficult to suppress – and actually demands to be lived out through our imagination.

[DJ– 0] Seeds, 2000. Stainless steel, gold-plated

Annäherung 3

Lassen wir uns führen von der Verweigerung der in Augenschein genommenen ‚Gegenstände', die sich nicht mit gewohnter Routine abhandeln lassen. Neugierig auf unerwartete Denkräume, vertiefen wir unsere ersten Wahrnehmungen und erweitern unseren Blickwinkel auf Zuordnungen, Eigenschaften, Wertungen: das Metall – kein warmes Gold, aber auch kein Silber – eigentlich grau, glatt, kalt, spiegelnd.

Wir erfahren: es handelt sich um medizinischen Stahl. Stahl – dessen sprichwörtliche Präzision wird uns bewusst. Medizinisch – inhaltliche Konnotationen entstehen: antiseptisch, klinisch, technisch, kühl,existenziell – . Eigene, erinnerte Erfahrungen begleiten den für uns relevanten Ausdruck. Fühlen wir uns von dem Ausdrucksraum des Materials seltsam berührt?

Fragen wir uns: lag etwas vergleichbar Irritierendes schon in der Form? Oder überwog ein Bedürfnis/die Neugier, die Form zwischen den Fingern zu bewegen, abzutasten, und im Spiel mehr über das „Ding" und die eigene Hand zu erfahren? Analogien zum eigenen Körper zu suchen, seinen Ort unter der Haut zu finden?

Wir entdecken: Material und Form in ihren wechselseitigen Relationen.

Interim 2

Wenn genaues Sehen und Lesen, noch ein rationaler Vorgang zu sein scheint, so bewegt sich die Wahrnehmung von Formen, Materialien und der Relationen der Phänomene untereinander deutlich weniger in festgelegten berechenbaren Bahnen. Es sind sinnlich empfundene Hinweise auf Gesehenes, Erfahrenes, sie stellen Denkräume für unsere Assoziationen her.

Auf welche Gedankenwege führt uns das Material Leder? Ungefärbtes Naturleder. Auch hier ist unsere Erinnerung gefragt, assoziieren wir Hilfskonstruktion, orthopädisches Zubehör, Orthesen, Hilfsmittel für den Bewegungsapparat? Oder: eine Hundeleine, den Schulranzen, ein Sportgerät, eine Waffe? Wieder entsteht durch die Wechselwirkung von Form und Material angestoßen eine starke emotionale Komponente, die durch Alltagsroutine schwerer zu überblenden ist – geradezu fordert, von unserer Vorstellungskraft durchlebt zu werden.

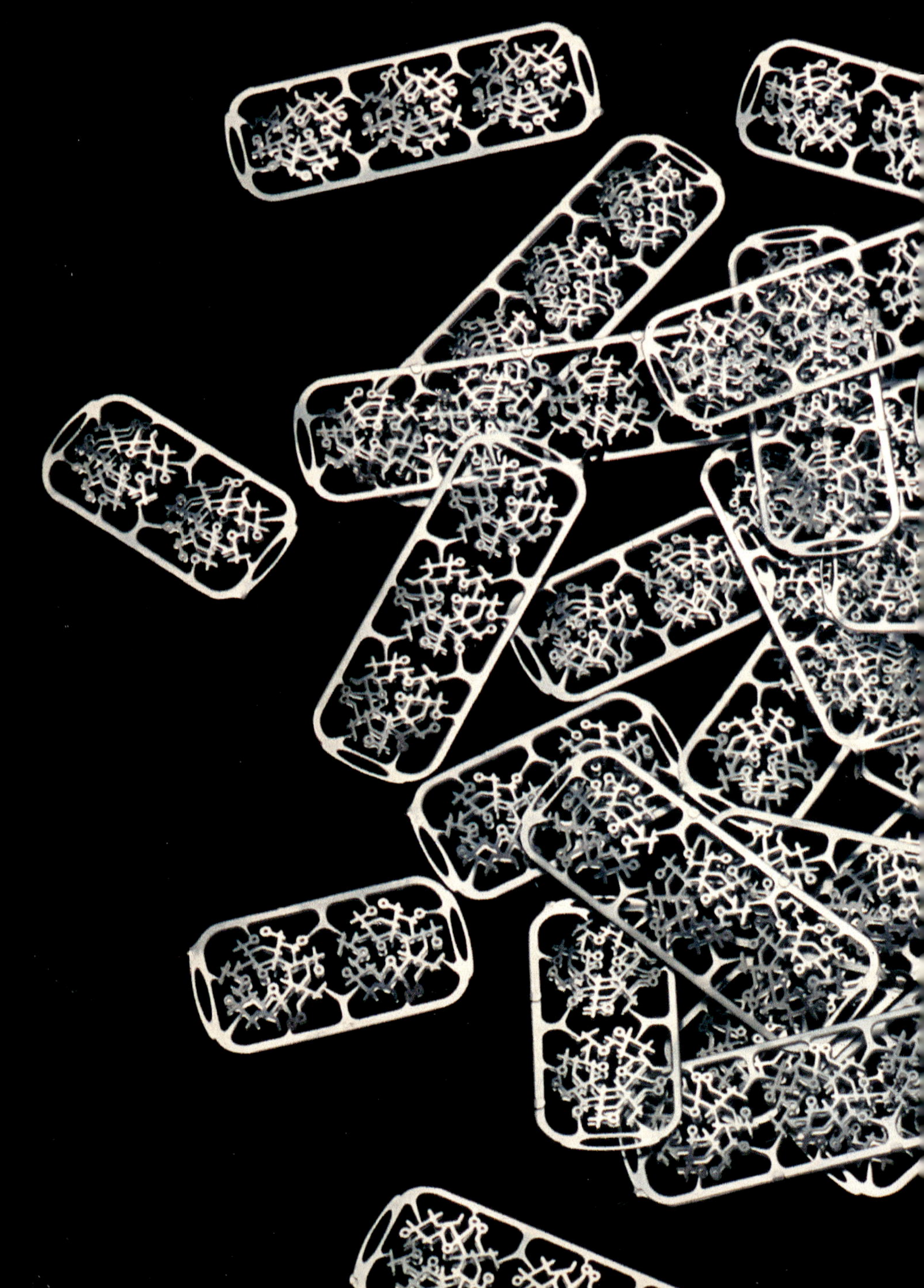

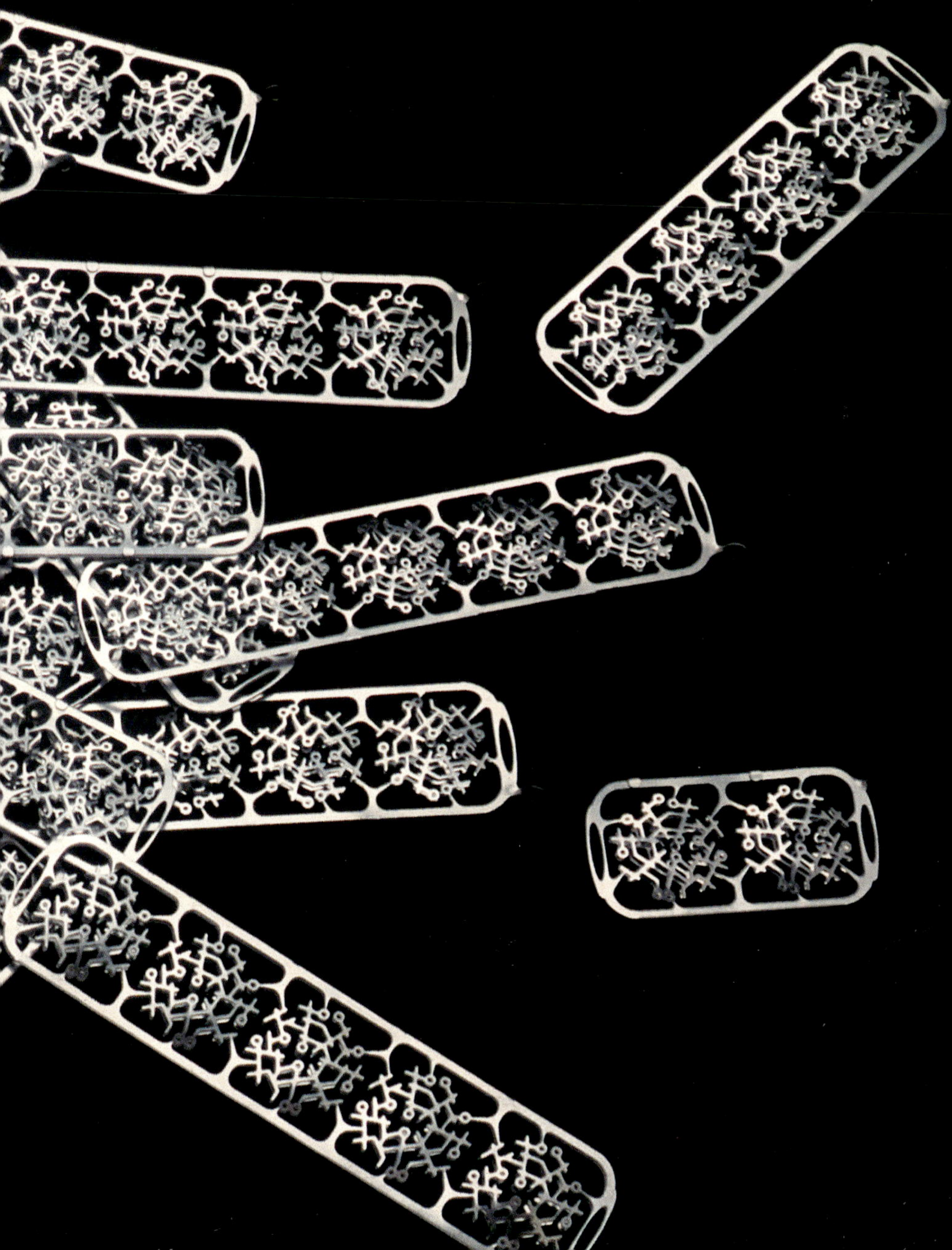

[DJ-00]

Approach 4

Let's give in to our associations by the beholding of a *Relic Rosé*, whose pale pink oscillates between skin and panty hose, whose downy surface could just as well be a delicate infestation of mildew like precious velvet. [13]

And the form? [14]

Our correlation of the forms balances in an unusual way between identification of particular bones, which could be seen as comparable to our own skeleton…

… and combinations of bones, whose arrangement suggests unusual unknown forms and triggers equally as unusual associations. [15]

Finally it remains for us as well to think about the inexplicableness of the origin, to feel all the implications of an Ossarium Rosé, an "ossuary in pink".

The Last / First Step – Handle, Try On

In the close-to-the-skin, inescapable dialogue with ourselves, [with] our skeleton, we notice how the perception of the form, the sensibility for the materiality do not only follow rational ways.

"body pieces" "foreign body" "body supports" "relic rosé"

We realize, how the imagination is ignited by the literal allusions of the naming [which functions] between word signal and message, and an amazing terrain of sensual sensibilities is opened up for us - emotions arise, whose interpretation is not yet possessed by habits.

On our body the artificially manufactured distance melts and gives way to an urge to carry the innermost outwards. This feeling puts the [particularly] shaped-by-our-times perception of life and death into question. Absorbed we stand before a confrontation with our cool way of dealing with death, feel the hurdle of dying as taboo and the inevitability of transience. We do not find any answers as to why, how and to what end, but the questions... **SR**

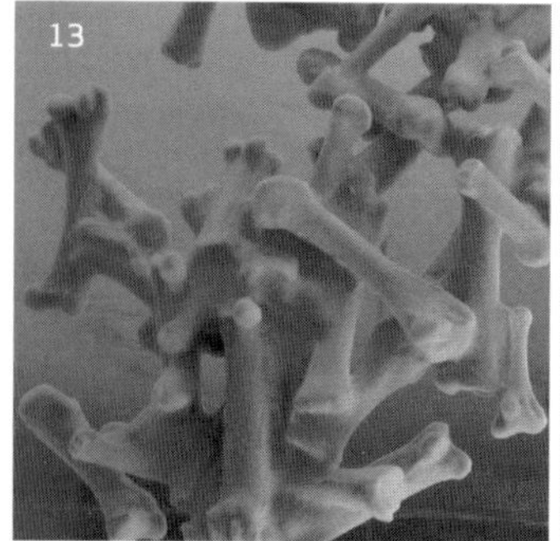
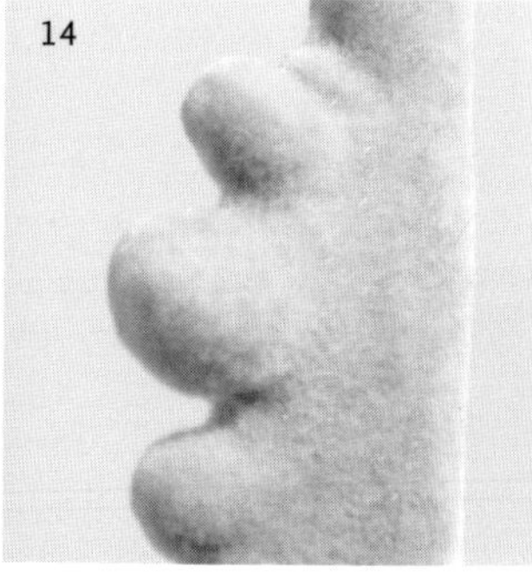
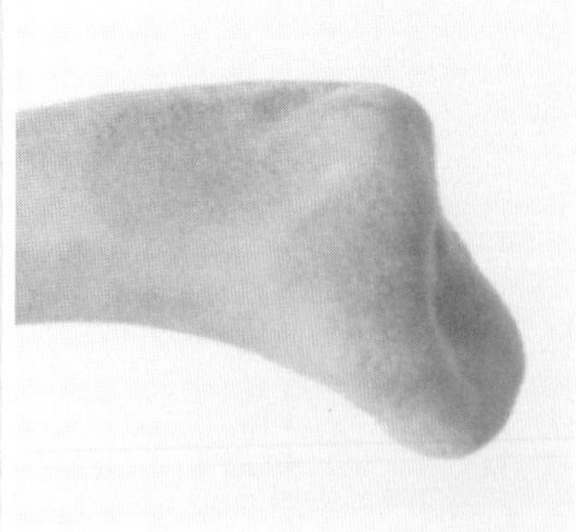

[DJ–00] Data Jewels, 1999. Stainless steel, computer generated drawing

Annäherung 4

Überantworten wir uns unseren Assoziationen beim Anblick eines *Relic Rosé*, dessen blasses Rosa zwischen Haut und Strumpfhose oszilliert, dessen flaumige Oberfläche ebenso ein feiner Schimmelbefall wie kostbarer Samt sein könnte. [13]

Und die Form? [14]

Unsere Zuordnung der Formen balanciert auf seltsame Weise zwischen Identifikation einzelner Knochen, die vergleichend zu unserem eigenen Skelett gesehen werden können ... [15]

... und Knochen-Kombinationen, deren Zusammenstellung seltsame unbekannte Formen hervorbringt und ebenso seltsame Assoziationen auslöst.

Letztlich bleibt es uns überlassen auch noch über das Ungeklärte der Herkunft nachzudenken, alle Implikationen eines *Ossarium Rosé*, eines „Beinhauses in Rosa" zu erfühlen.

Der letzte / erste Schritt – in die Hand nehmen, sich anlegen

Im hautnahen, unausweichlichen Dialog mit uns selbst, unserem Skelett, bemerken wir, wie sich die Wahrnehmung der Form, das Empfinden für die Materialität nicht allein in rationalen Bahnen bewegt.

„body pieces" „fremdkörper" „body supports" „relic rosé"

Wir stellen fest, wie sich die Vorstellungskraft an sprachlichen Anspielungen der Namensgebung zwischen Wortsignal und Botschaft entzündet, und sich ein erstaunliche Terrain der sinnlichen Empfindungen für uns öffnet – Emotionen entstehen, deren Deutung noch nicht durch Gewohnheiten besetzt sind.

Auf unserem Körper schmilzt die künstlich hergestellt Distanz und weicht einem Gefühl, Innerstes nach Außen zu tragen. Dieses Gefühl stellt die von dieser, unserer Zeit geprägte Wahrnehmung von Leben und Tod in Frage. Gelenkt stehen wir vor einer Auseinandersetzung mit unserem coolen Umgang mit dem Tod, fühlen die Hürde des Sterbens als Tabu und das Unausweichliche der Vergänglichkeit. Wir finden keine Antworten auf ein Warum, Wie und Wohin, aber die Fragen ...

Dr. Phil. Sabine Runde
Stellvertretende Direktorin und Kuratorin
für Angewandte Kunst 20. + 21. Jh.
Museum für Angewandte Kunst Frankfurt.

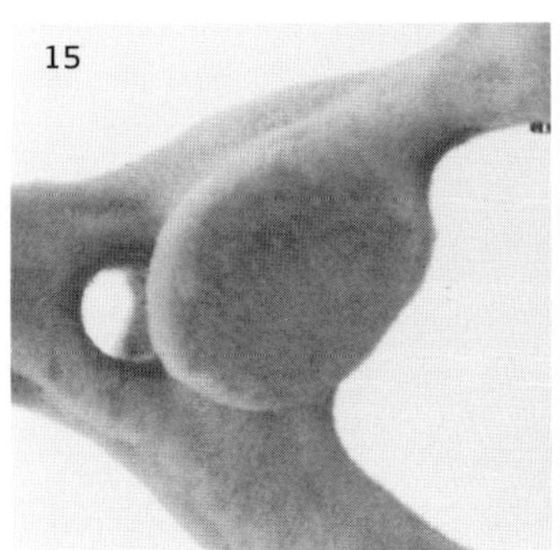
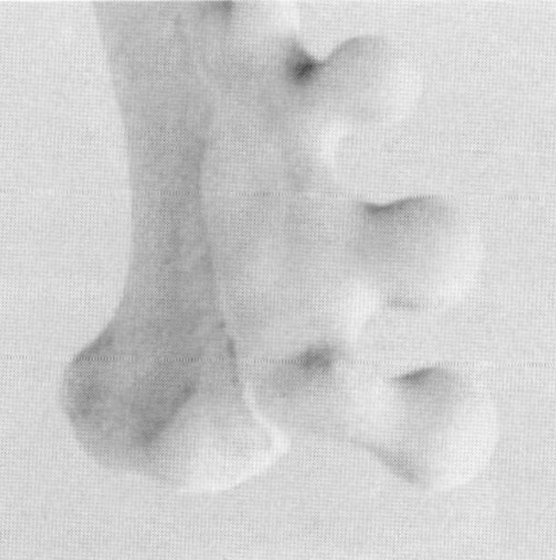
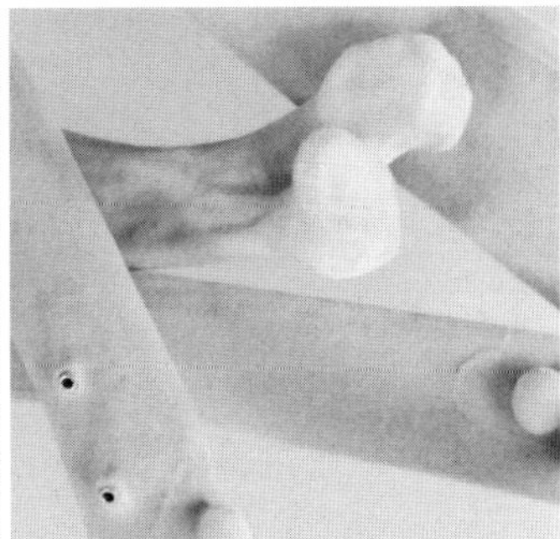

[PW–00] Fisch holding **Seed**, 2003. Porcelain ⊢──

[PW-00]

In the age of post-modernity the reassessment of all values has become a matter of routine. Naturally this also applies to human embodiment and the body per se. Today proclamations of future spectacular metamorphoses of the body's inner constitution and its outer appearance are innumerable, in particular, in the depths and shallows of the Internet. Examples of modifications of the body which evidence the desire for radical alternation and optimisation of the natural body through *Körperdesign* ['body design'] have become impossible to ignore: anti-aging programs, liposuction, plastic surgery promising eternal youth and which also transforms ugly ducklings into swans in front of live-TV cameras, sex changes, organ transplants and so-called organ breeding, pre-natal diagnostics, and the first prospects of being able to assure absolute health in the distant future through the wonders of the biotechnological industry. Not forgetting the cyborgs and virtual doubles of those humans who, interconnected in the Internet today via broadband technology, engage in respective role-playing games and thereby lead a 'second life' which in certain circumstances rewards and means far more to them than their first, in which, as conventional beings of flesh and blood, they barely manage to eke out an existence.

In recent decades in society the readiness to reach for invasive procedures and means of influencing the human body and its appearance seems to have drastically increased. This could also confirm the assumption that ways of human self-modification and perfectionism which still resort to accessories, 'appendages' and 'extensions', i.e., the most various kinds of adorning the body, are retrograde, have long ago already become anachronistic – indeed, the very idea of the integrity of the human body itself has long since become antiquated and obsolete, at most, is only of nostalgic value.

Christoph Zellweger's jewellery works do not suggest the contrary, but they sharpen the view: the actual scene of human self-transformation is not its physique, even if this is actually of undreamed plasticity, but rather the world of its imagination. Thereby Zellweger demonstrates: A piece of jewellery behaves in relation to the human body like a prosthetic joint behaves in relation to the skeletal structure – it is the prosthesis-like function of jewellery which especially engages Zellweger. Jewellery has a socio-cultural function, body-adornment serves communication. It is an aid that shifts the functional body towards a body of meaning. Zellweger sees the human being as *homo ipsi faber* [1]; i.e. as a human, who strives to invent himself; a being, whose transformational fantasy and imagination overshadows what even its most advanced and boldest technologies of modification and self-change are able to reach. It is undisputed: the human body will

PM–T[42-59]

Jewellery as Prostheses

Body design in bio-political discourse

Dr. Pietro Morandi

Associate Professor at the HgkZ, University of the Arts Zurich, Institute of Cultural Studies in Art, Media and Design; adjunct professor (political theory) at the University of Potsdam

[PW–000] Brains, 2001. Porcelain

Schmuck als Prothese
Körperdesign im bio-politischen Diskurs

Die Umwertung aller Werte ist im Zeitalter
der Nach-Moderne längst Routine geworden.
Selbstverständlich gilt dies auch für den
menschlichen Leib und Körper. Ankündi-
gungen künftiger spektakulärer Metamor-
phosen seiner inneren Verfassung und seines
äusseren Erscheinungsbildes finden sich
heute ohne Zahl, insbesondere in den Tiefen
und Untiefen des Internets. Unübersehbar
sind die Beispiele geworden, die den Wunsch
nach tiefgreifender Veränderung und Opti-
mierung des ‚Körperdesigns‘ dokumentieren:
Anti-Aging-Programm, Fettabsaugung,
eine ewige Jugend verheissende plastische
Chirurgie, die auch vor laufender TV-Kamera
hässliche Entlein in Schwäne verwandelt,
Geschlechtsumwandlungen, Organtransplan-
tation und Organnachzüchtung, pränatale
Diagnostik und die erst für eine fernere
Zukunft in Aussicht gestellten Gesundheits-
versprechen der Biotechnologie-Branche.
Nicht zu vergessen auch die Cyborgs und
virtuellen Doppelgänger jener Menschen, die
heute im Internet durch Breitbandtechno-
logie vernetzt in einschlägigen Rollenspielen
ein ‚zweites Leben‘ führen, das ihnen unter
Umständen weit mehr einträgt und bedeutet
als ihr erstes, das sie noch immer als konventionelle Wesen aus Fleisch und Blut fristen.
Generell scheint die Bereitschaft in der
Gesellschaft in den letzten Jahrzehnten
drastisch gestiegen zu sein, nach invasiven
Verfahren und Mitteln der Beeinflussung des
menschlichen Körpers und dessen Erscheinungsbildes zu greifen. Dies könnte auch die
Vermutung nähren, dass Verfahren mensch-

licher Selbstveränderung und Perfektionie-
rung, die noch auf *accessories*, ‚Anhängsel‘
und ‚Anbauten‘, unterschiedlichster Art
basieren, längst ausgedient haben – ja, daß
die Idee der Integrität des menschlichen
Körpers selbst antiquiert und obsolet
geworden ist. Sie ist allenfalls noch von
nostalgischem Wert.

Christoph Zellwegers Schmuck-Arbeiten
behaupten nichts Gegenteiliges, sie schärfen
aber den Blick: der eigentliche Schauplatz
menschlicher Selbsttransformation ist nicht
dessen Physis, auch wenn diese tatsächlich
von ungeahnter Plastizität ist, sondern
dessen Vorstellungswelt. Dabei zeigt Zellweger: Das Schmuckstück verhält sich
zum menschlichen Körper etwa so wie eine
Gelenkprothese zum Knochenbau – es ist die
Prothesen-ähnliche Funktion von Schmuck,
auf die es Zellweger besonders ankommt.
Schmuck hat eine sozio-kulturelle Funktion,
Körperschmuck dient der Kommunikation,
ist ein Hilfsmittel das die Körperfunktion
in Richtung Bedeutungsfunktion erweitert.
Zellweger sieht den Menschen als *homo ipsi
faber* [1]; als einen Menschen also, der sich
selbst erfinden will; ein Wesen, dessen trans-
formative Phantasie und Vorstellungskraft in
den Schatten stellen, was selbst seine avan-
ciertesten und kühnsten Technologien der
Veränderungen und Selbstveränderung zu
erreichen vermögen. Es ist unbestritten: Der
menschliche Körper wird zunehmend nicht
nur als funktional ‚limitiert‘, als unzureichend
schön, als mangelhaft und nicht zufrieden-
stellend interpretiert, sondern auch tatsächlich verändert. Da sollen die neuen Technologien einspringen um erhöhten Erwartungen
zu befriedigen. Aber schaffen sie es?

1. *homo ipsi faber* [der Mensch der sich selbst (er)schafft; *homo faber* (zu deutsch etwa: der schaffende Mensch oder
der menschliche Handwerker) *ipsi* (selbst)]; Begriff den Zellweger erstmals 1996 in einem Vortrag auf Einladung vom
British Crafts Council im BDC London-Islington anläßlich der Ausstellung ‚New Times New Thinking‘ gebraucht. Redner
auf Konferenz: Gianpaolo Babetto (I), Bernhard Schobinger (CH), Fred Woell (USA), Christoph Zellweger (UK/CH).

0008830
0008250

not only be increasingly interpreted as functionally 'limited', as insufficiently beautiful, as defective and unsatisfactory, but also actually modified. It is here where new technologies should come to the rescue to fulfil our heightened expectations. But do they succeed?

Let's take an exemplary survey. Aren't we somewhat disappointed that the 'new technologies', for example, medical implants, can still usually only repair or preserve, but not completely replace, extend or exceed human organs? Aren't we disappointed about the fact that the idea to set up an interface between human brains and computers has turned out to be purely hot-air – just like all the other promises of eternal youth? Aren't we disappointed about the fact that medications produced on the basis of genetic-technologies have by no means yet made conventional forms of therapy obsolete, that common pharmaceuticals, such as antibiotics or aspirin, have not long since been surpassed and that the facelift doesn't promise permanent beauty, the breast reduction – or, respectively, breast enlargement, as the case may be – no longer promise personal bliss? In short: Aren't we disappointed about the fact that reality always lags behind our imagination?

Tongue in cheek Zellweger invites us to deal with our overpowering imagination as a key 'problem' of humanity, with our sense of possibility. Today the human body is at the centre of attention. In this context, what is commonly referred to as 'jewellery' as a means of adorning the body has become an important special case among culturally significant prostheses. Obviously possessing an incorrigible tendency towards self-metamorphosis, human nature not only cultivates a world-creating sense of reality, but also a no less world-producing sense of possibility. Its exorbitant fantasies cannot be sobered by such a still-so-limited ability of realisation. Zellweger's objects illuminate this context and also make a contribution in their own way to anthropological basic research, to the analytics of human imagination and, above all, to the self-assuredness of *homo ipsi faber*.

Zellweger's objects, often produced with the highest technical precision, evoke multiple associations to precious reliquaries, burial objects, found objects from a possible future, and they thereby show again and again what remains of a human when one is laid to grave: it is not its body, but much rather its prostheses – it is a matter here of bone implants, artificial dentures or also even of jewellery-burial objects – all of them artefacts, which are kneaded from the same dough of an almost compulsory will to *Gestalten*, i.e., to design. These objects formulate an anthropological thesis: ultimately humans strive as *homo protheticus* [2] after prostheses against aging, after the attainment of immortality. Is the actual motive of this compulsion of self-design a striving after omnipotence, an expression of human narcissism – or is it not true at

1. *homo ipsi faber* / the human who is the creator of (him)self, [*homo faber* ('man the smith' or 'man the maker') *ipsi* (self)]. Term which Zellweger first used in 1996 in a lecture upon an invitation of the British Crafts Council at the BDC London-Islington on the occasion of the exhibition ,New Times New Thinking'. Conference Speakers: Gianpaolo Babetto (I), Bernhard Schobinger (CH), Fred Woell (USA), Christoph Zellweger (UK/CH).

2. Arnold Gehlen; *Der Mensch. Seine Natur und seine Stellung in der Welt*. Berlin 1940.

[FB–000] Foreign Bodies #0008720, #0008250 and #0008150, 2003. Medical stainless steel, bones

Machen wir die Probe aufs Exempel. Sind
wir etwa nicht darüber enttäuscht, dass die
‚neuen Technologien', beispielsweise medi-
zinische Implantate, menschliche Organe
noch immer meist nur reparieren oder
erhalten, nicht aber umfassend ersetzen,
erweitern oder übertreffen können? Sind wir
nicht enttäuscht darüber, daß sich die Idee,
eine Schnittstelle zwischen menschlichen
Gehirnen und Computern einzurichten, als
reine Schaumschlägerei entpuppt – ebenso
wie alle anderen Versprechen auf ewige
Jugend? Sind wir nicht enttäuscht darüber,
daß auf gentechnologischer Basis erstellte
Medikamente herkömmliche Therapieformen
noch keineswegs haben obsolet werden
lassen, dass vertraute Wirkstoffe wie Anti-
biotika oder Aspirin nicht längst überboten
wurden und dass das Facelift nicht perma-
nente Schönheit, die Brustverkleinerung
bzw. -vergrößerung nicht zwingend mehr
persönliches Glück verspricht? Kurzum: Sind
wir etwa nicht darüber enttäuscht, daß die
Realität stets hinter unserer Imagination
zurückbleibt?

Zellweger fordert uns augenzwinkernd
dazu auf, uns mit unserer übermächtigen
Imagination als einem zentralen ‚Problem'
des Menschen zu beschäftigen, mit unserem
Möglichkeitssinn. Der menschliche Körper
steht heute im Zentrum der Aufmerksamkeit
und in diesem Zusammenhang ist auch jener
Spezialfall unter den kulturell signifikanten
Prothesen von zentraler Bedeutung, die für
gewöhnlich als ‚Schmuck' bezeichnet werden.
Die menschliche Natur, die so offensichtlich
über eine unverbesserliche Selbstverwand-
lungsneigung verfügt, bildet neben einem
weltschaffenden Realitätssinn auch einen
nicht minder welterzeugenden Möglichkeitssinn aus. Dessen überschiessende
Phantasien können von keinem auch noch
so beschränkten Realisierungsvermögen
ernüchtert werden. Zellwegers Objekte
erhellen diesen Zusammenhang und leisten
auf ihre Weise auch einen Beitrag zur anthro-
pologischen Grundlagenforschung, zur
Analytik menschlicher Imagination und vor
allem zur Selbstvergewisserung des *homo
ipsi faber.*

Zellwegers Objekte, oft mit höchster tech-
nischer Präzision gearbeitet, evozieren vielfach Erinnerungen an kostbare Reliquiare,
an Grabbeigaben, an Fundstücke aus einer
möglichen Zukunft, und sie zeigen dabei
immer wieder, was vom Menschen übrig
bleibt, wenn er zu Grabe gelegt wird: es ist
nicht sein Leib, wohl aber seine Prothesen,
handle es sich hierbei um Knochenim-
plantate, Zahnprothesen oder eben auch
Schmuck-Grabbeigaben – allesamt Arte-
fakte, die aus demselben Teig eines geradezu
zwanghaften Gestaltungswillens geknetet
sind. Diese Objekte formulieren die anthro-

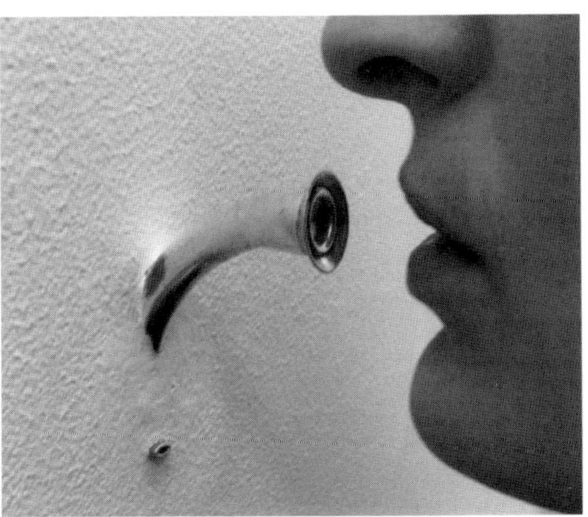

Breath piece, 2005. Silver
Second hand tracheotomy-breathing device

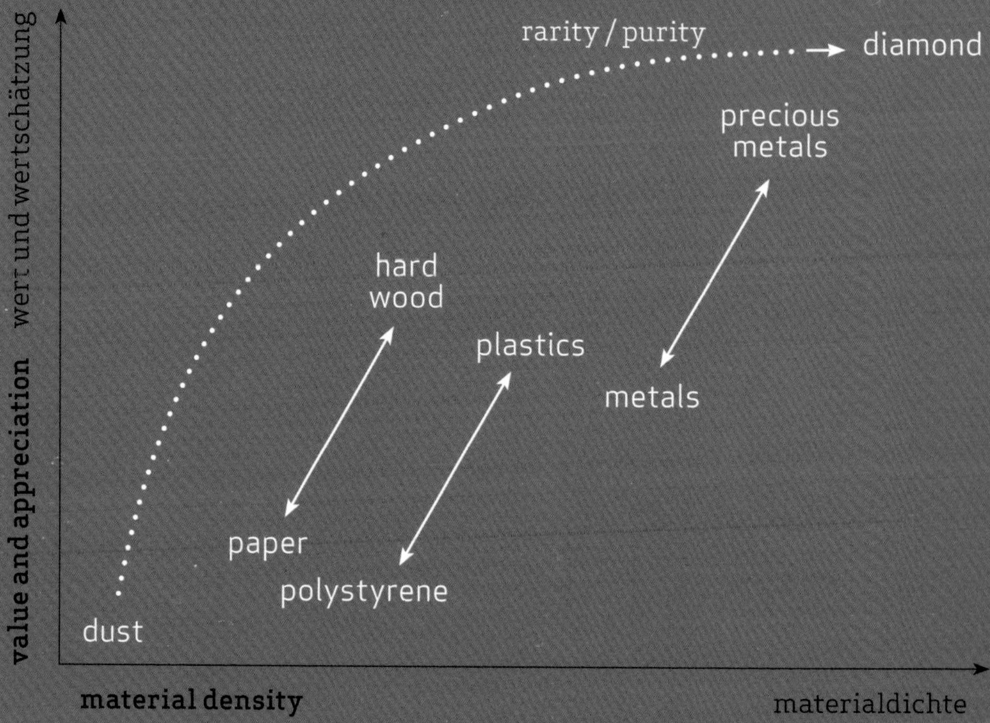

fig 1: MATERIAL chart: the more dense a material the higher its value

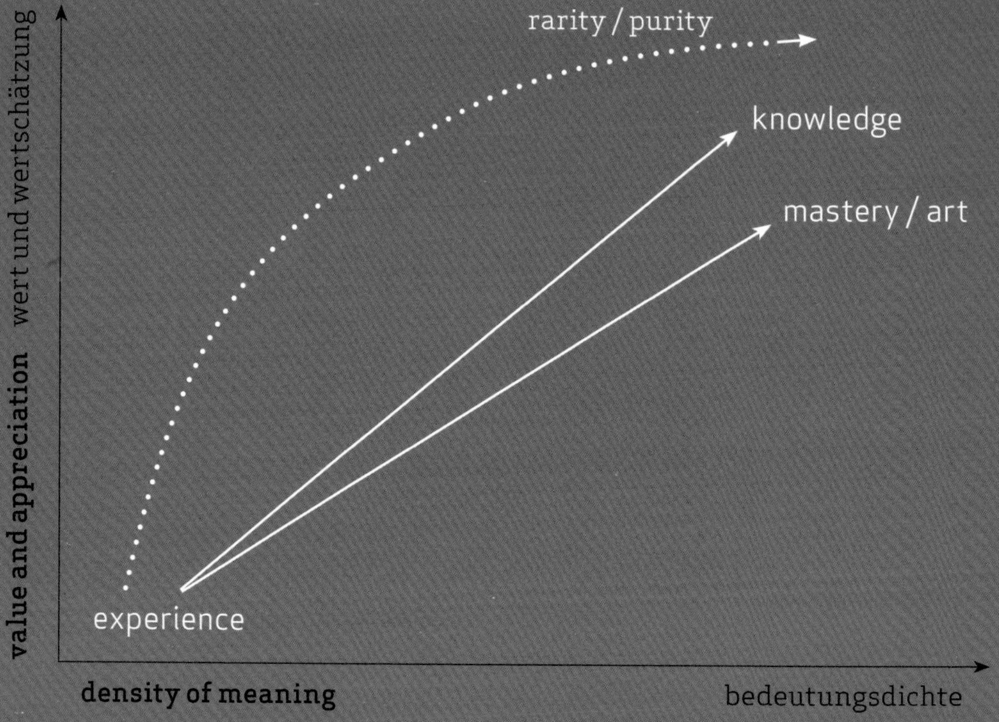

fig 2: INFORMATION chart: condensed information increases meaning

[BP-00]

all that humans want to live eternally, but rather that they simply do not want to die, as was once formulated by the science fiction satirist Stanislaw Lem?

Zellweger also gives descriptive diagrams and tables (to those who ask) to take along with his objects and artefacts. Often these are articulated with an almost mathematical precision. This accompanying material shows that Zellweger is a scientist among designers and artists, at times with a bias for meticulous calculation. In such a graphic form we then see, for example, an exact correlation between 'value', 'appreciation' and physical density of substances, of materials, like wood or metal, which differ in weight and thereby also differ in their degree of preciousness and worth. As a result, questions arise: in terms of its value and its significance, what actually is the counterpart to a piece of jewellery made out of gold or stainless steel? The answer: a piece of jewellery made out of polystyrene. What do those adorning themselves with precious metal jewellery betray to us? What do those wearing a 'commodity chain' out of polystyrene tell us about their value system? This is where the investigation of meaning – and, thereby, also of the content of art – takes place.

Born as Proteus, today's human is often also entangled in its own auto-manipulations in a completely involuntary way. Today's human sometimes loses itself completely in the endless play of its deceptions and, above all, its self-deceptions. Manmade extensions of itself make it difficult, if not impossible, to clearly distinguish between a foreign body and its own body. A wide grey zone stretches between complete acceptance and complete rejection of a prosthesis. Jewellery is a body extension which oscillates on multiple levels between foreign body and ones own body and thereby raises the questions: how do plaidoyers, i.e., social norms arise? What do bodily integrity and the integrity of identity mean? How far can a human being go in determining its own body and its identity?

Indeed plastic surgery exactly demonstrates just how narrow the degree is between the seemingly necessary and the superfluous, a range, which is an intense concern of Zellweger. A crooked nose caused by an accident is 'restored' – a congenital 'crooked' nose, however, is designed 'anew'. As jewellery maker, Zellweger has a tradition behind him that deals with issues of identity and the formation of identity, with status, symbolism

Shopping, Malta, 1995

Advertising, London Underground, 2006

[BP–00] Body Piece V11, 1997. Expanded polystyrene

pologische These: der Mensch strebt als
homo protheticus [2] letztlich nach einer
Prothese gegen das Altern, nach Erlangung
von Unsterblichkeit. Ist das eigentliche
Motiv dieses Selbstgestaltungsdrangs ein
Streben nach Allmacht, ein Ausdruck von
menschlichem Narzissmus – oder ist es
gar nicht so, daß die Menschen ewig leben,
sondern einfach nur nicht sterben wollen, wie
es einmal der Sciencefiction Satiriker Stanislaw Lem formuliert hat?

Seinen Objekten und Artefakten gibt
Zellweger (auf Anfrage) auch erläuternde
Diagramme und Tabellen mit auf den Weg.
Nicht selten werden diese in nahezu mathematischer Präzision formuliert. Diese Begleitunterlagen zeigen, daß Zellweger unter den
Gestaltern und Künstlern ein Wissenschaftler
ist, mit Hang zu zuweilen akribischem
Vermessen. Wir sehen dann beispielsweise
eine in grafische Form gebrachte exakte
Korrelation zwischen ‚Wert‘, ‚Wertschätzung‘ und physikalischer Dichte von Stoffen,
von Materialien wie den unterschiedlich
schweren, und damit auch unterschiedlich
edlen und wertvollen Hölzern oder Metallen.
Daraus ergeben sich Fragestellungen: Was ist
eigentlich in seinem Wert und seiner Wertigkeit das Gegenstück zu einem Schmuckstück
aus Gold oder edlem Stahl? Die Antwort: Ein
Schmuckstück aus Styropor. Was verraten
uns die Träger und Trägerinnen von Edelmetallschmuck? Was verrät uns die Trägerin
einer *Waren-Kette* aus Styropor über ihren
Wertekanon? Hier findet die Auseinandersetzung mit Bedeutung statt und damit auch die
mit den Inhalten der Kunst.

Als geborener Proteus verstrickt sich der
heutige Mensch oft auch ganz unfreiwillig
in seinen Automanipulationen. Er verliert
sich zuweilen vollständig im unaufhörlichen
Spiel seiner Täuschungen und vor allem
Selbsttäuschungen. Die von ihm verfertigten
Extensionen seiner selbst machen es ihm
oft schwer, ja unmöglich, den Unterschied
zwischen Fremdkörper und Eigenkörper noch
klar zu sehen. Zwischen vollständiger Anverwandlung und vollständiger Zurückweisung
einer Prothese erstreckt sich ein weites
Feld der Grautöne. Schmuck ist eine Körperextension, die vielfach oszilliert zwischen
Fremdkörper und Eigenkörper und damit
die Frage auslöst: Wie entstehen normative
Plädoyers? Was bedeutet körperliche Integrität und die Integrität von Identität? Wie
instrumentell kann und darf sich ein Mensch
überhaupt zu seinem Körper und seiner Identität verhalten?

Nun zeigt gerade die plastische Chirurgie,
ein Thema mit dem sich Zellweger intensiv
beschäftigt hat, wie schmal der Grat
zwischen scheinbar Notwendigem und
Überflüssigem ist. Eine unfallbedingt
schiefe Nase wird ‚wiederhergestellt‘ – eine
geburtsbedingt ‚schiefe‘ Nase hingegen
‚neu‘ gestaltet. Christoph Zellweger hat als
Schmuckmacher eine Tradition im Rücken,
die sich mit Identität und Identitätsbildung, mit Status, Symbolik und den damit
verbundenen Werten auseinanderstetzt.
Das Bedeutungsspektrum von Schmuck,
aber auch Schmucknarben, Tatoos, Mode und
Tracht, die in ständischen Gesellschaften die
Statusposition jedes einzelnen markierten,
werden nun durch neue Strategien erweitert.
Zu diesen gehören unter anderen auch die
invasiven Möglichkeiten des Körperdesigns.
Die Funktion des Funktionslosen muss vor

2. Arnold Gehlen, *Der Mensch. Seine Natur und seine Stellung in der Welt.* Berlin 1940.

[BP-000] Body Piece, 1998. Medical stainless steel, paint

[BP-000]

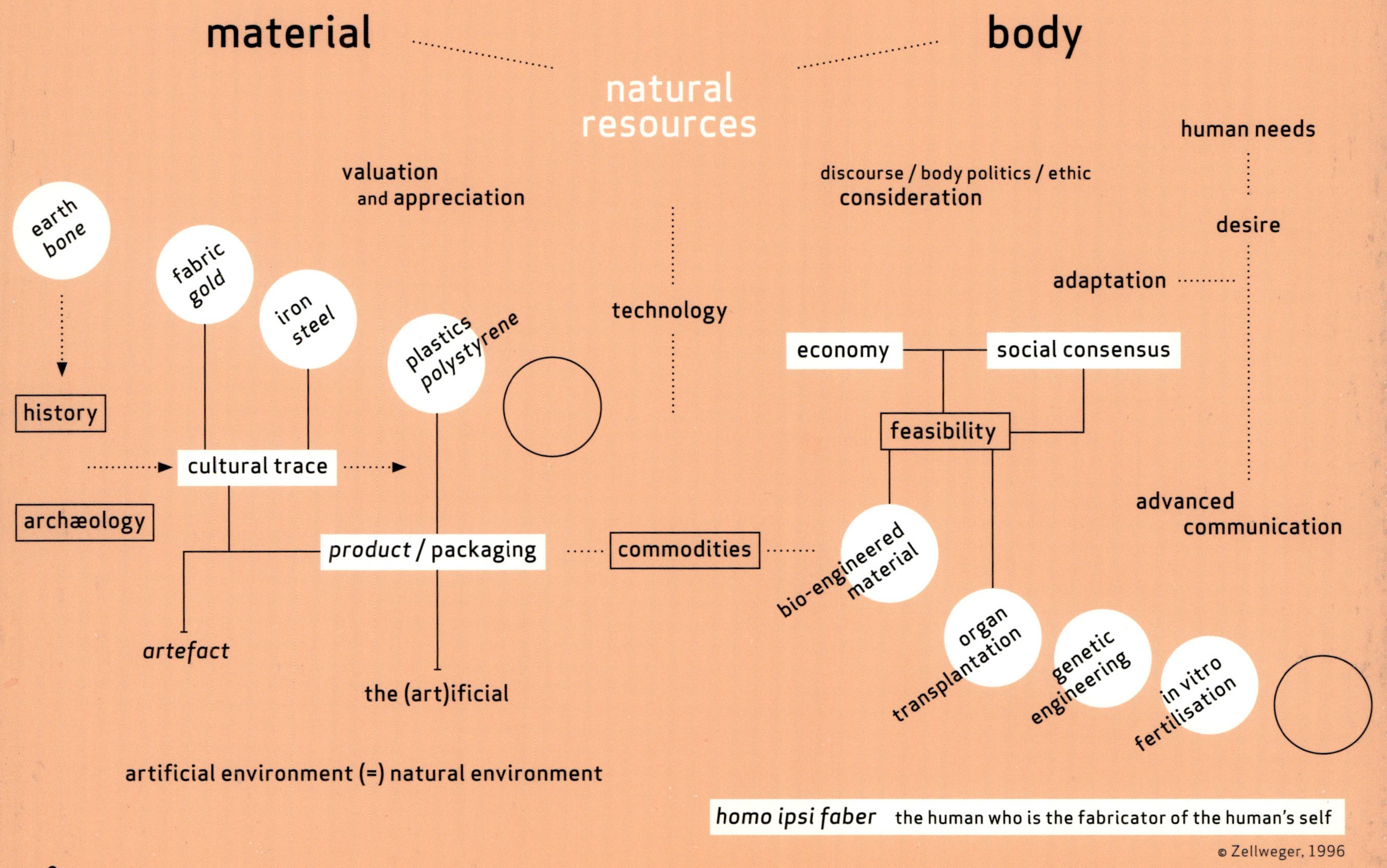

material

body

human needs

desire

natural resources

valuation and appreciation

discourse / body politics / ethic consideration

adaptation

social consensus

advanced communication

economy

feasibility

technology

bio-engineered material

commodities

organ transplantation

genetic engineering

in vitro fertilisation

homo ipsi faber   the human who is the fabricator of the human's self

© Zellweger, 1996

artificial environment (=) natural environment

the (art)ificial

product / packaging

plastics / polystyrene

cultural trace

steel / iron

fabric / gold

artefact

history

archæology

earth / bone

and associated values. The spectrum of meanings of jewellery, as well as adornment cutting and scarring, tattoos, fashion, and folk costumes, which in hierarchical societies traditionally mark the social rank of each individual, have been extended through new strategies. Along with other means, these also include, the invasive possibilities of bodily modification or so-called 'body design'. The function of the non-functional has to be considered further against the background of the newly available technologies that aim to directly design the body, in the sense of the function of adornment, in a lasting – rather than temporary – way.

For followers of modernism jewellery implied 'traditionalism' – and traditionalists since the 19th century have frequently practiced an anti-modernistic critic of functionalism and thereby also often emphasized the special status and merit of the seemingly non-functional. That is, functionalism criticizes traditionalism and vice versa. But how relevant is this conflict still? One of many possible conceivable ways out of this discourse deadlock of overly simplistic binary distinctions can be detected in the anthropology of Arnold Gehlen and his bio-sociological and bio-political concepts, which met with considerable approval in the 1950s and 1960s in German-speaking countries, but today, however, are hardly known. Gehlen as well as Zellweger seem to follow similar anthropologies, which understand humans as *homo protheticus*, admittedly with the difference that Gehlen does not leave the modern notion of function behind, but rather he radically intensifies it and – although involuntarily – carries it to *ad absurdum*. For Gehlen the human being is 'defective' or 'lacking'. Notoriously it suffers from deficits in adapting to its natural environment. The human body is unspecialised. It is not particularly well-adapted to any ecological niche and for this reason is rather dependent on prostheses, which make this adaptation possible for it, an adaptation which its natural biological endowment doesn't provide for. Thereby this 'lacking being' unavoidably transforms itself into a 'prostheses animal'. It produces, for example, knives or rifles, to compensate for the lack of well-fortified teeth; clothing or heating devices because it lacks a warming pelt; magnifying glasses or telescopes, which increase its power of sight; and, wheels or airplanes, in order to increase its mobility. Although other animals also produce and use prostheses, for example, as tools, yet in comparison to humans these seem more subsidiary, as simple reinforcement of bodily functions.

Homo protheticus is not only open for organ reinforcement and other comparatively superficial optimisations and means of perfectionism, but for fundamental transformations for which there is no longer any certain predestined direction of adaptation. Against this background ones own and the foreign body become indistinguishable, their distinction doesn't arise automatically any longer of itself, but, when necessary, from now on has to be made consciously and legitimised.

Homo Ipsi Faber–chart, 1996

dem Hintergrund der neu anwendbaren Technologien, die den Körper direkt, im Sinne der Schmuckfunktion, nachhaltig zu gestalten vermögen, weitergedacht werden.

Für Anhänger der Moderne implizierte Schmuck ‚Traditionalismus' – und Traditionalisten haben seit dem 19. Jahrhundert vielfach antimodernistische Funktionalismuskritik geübt und dabei oft auch die besondere Würde des scheinbar Funktionslosen hervorgehoben. Der Funktionalismus kritisiert also den Traditionalismus und vice versa. Wie relevant ist dieser Konflikt noch? Einer von vielen denkbaren möglichen Auswegen aus eingefahrenen Diskursgeleisen dieser allzu simplen binären Unterscheidung lässt sich in der Anthropologie Arnold Gehlens und dessen biosoziologische und biopolitische Konzepte aufspüren, die in den 1950 und 1960er Jahren im deutschsprachigen Raum erhebliche Resonanz gefunden hat, heute aber kaum noch öffentlich präsent ist. Gehlen wie Zellweger scheinen ähnlichen Anthropologien zu folgen, die den Menschen als *homo protheticus* auffasst, mit dem Unterschied freilich, daß Gehlen den modernen Funktionsbegriff nicht hinter sich lässt, sondern vielmehr radikalisiert und, wenn auch unfreiwillig, ad absurdum führt. Für Gehlen ist der Mensch ein ‚Mängelwesen'. Notorisch leidet es unter Anpassungsdefiziten an seine natürliche Lebensumwelt. Der menschliche Körper ist unspezialisiert. Er ist an keine ökologische Nische besonders gut angepasst und daher stets auf Prothesen angewiesen, die ihm jene Anpassung ermöglichen, die ihm seine natürliche biologische Ausstattung verweigert. Daher transformiert sich dieses Mängelwesen zwangs-

läufig in ein ‚Prothesen-Tier'. Es verfertigt beispielsweise Messer oder Gewehre, die an die Stelle fehlender wehrhafter Zähne treten und Kleider oder Heizapparate, weil es über kein wärmendes Fell verfügt, Lupen oder Fernrohre, die seine Sehkraft steigern und Räder oder Flugzeuge, um seine Mobilität zu erhöhen. Zwar verfertigen und nutzen auch andere Tiere Prothesen, beispielsweise Werkzeuge, doch wirken diese im Vergleich zum Menschen subsidiär, als einfache Verstärkung von Körperfunktionen.

Homo protheticus ist nicht nur offen für Organverstärkung und andere vergleichsweise oberflächliche Optimierungen und Perfektionierungen, sondern für fundamentale Transformationen, denen keine bestimmte Anpassungsrichtung mehr vorgegeben ist. Vor diesem Hintergrund werden auch Eigen- und Fremdkörper ununterscheidbar, ihre Distinktion ergibt sich nicht mehr von selbst, sondern muss, falls unverzichtbar, nunmehr bewusst vorgenommen und legitimiert werden.

Bereits in den 1920er Jahren hat Sigmund Freud in seinem Aufsatz über das *„Unbehagen in der Kultur"* [3] den Menschen als einen ‚Prothesengott' charakterisiert, dessen wesentliches Motiv der Selbstveränderung der Wunsch nach Allmacht und Unsterblichkeit bildet. Die Kunstgeschichte überliefert seit frühester Zeit Bilder der Prothesenfertigung, die menschliche Hybris veranschaulichen sollen. So etwa den Flugapparat des Ikarus, aber auch die Errungenschaften der Schmiedekunst Hephaistos, der, obwohl hinkend, Prothesen stets nur für andere fertigte.

---

3. Sigmund Freud, „Das Unbehagen in der Kultur", in *Das Unbehagen in der Kultur und andere kulturtheoretische Schriften*, Fischer, 2001. (S.29-108).

[OR-00]

[OR-000] ●

Already in the 1920s in his essay 'Civilisation and Its Discontents' [3] Sigmund Freud characterized humans as a 'prosthetic God' whose essential aim of self-modification constitutes the desire for omnipotence and immortality. Since earliest times the history of art has provided images of the manufacturing of prostheses, whose aim is to depict human *hybris* as, for instance, the flying device of Icarus, as well as the accomplishments of the blacksmith artist Hephaestus, who despite his own limping, only produces prostheses for others.

Gehlen's prosthetics doctrine goes beyond this tradition. For him prostheses constitute and represent the created, the artificial and the available, which are the contrary of the natural as a total of everything non-artificial and not available. 'Culture' itself is advanced by Gehlen as equal to a prosthesis; as an artificial nature of the second order; and, as an instrument of adaptation, positioned between the 'lacking' human being and its primordial natural environment. This second artificial world itself creates the *homo protheticus* in its characteristic qualities more as born 'artist' or rather prostheses-maker than as one who proves itself socially and politically.

After this further explanation of the 'prosthetics' of Gehlen, it should now be possible to more closely determine the prosthetic status of 'adornment' and thereby its special functionality as an element of culture:

Jewellery reduces the work of human adaptation. The use of adornment serves to relieve communication: setting the course, it puts filtering premises or assumptions in place; it facilitates the opening and leading of desired, fertile discussions and processes of communication; and, it prevents the occasion of unwanted contact. Jewellery thereby has an impact upon the position towards the self as well as the position towards others, communication with others. It may also cause self-manipulation and the manipulation of third parties. In the 21st century, as Zellweger extends the term, *jewellery as prostheses* is also making an impact and often particularly so when it is worn concealed, i.e., on or even within the body, because now the body itself has become the thing to be designed; the body has become jewellery.

Thereby, like the entire human production of prostheses, jewellery – as it is conventionally understood – is gradually leaving the stage of organ reinforcement and organ accentuation behind. No more an *accessio* i.e., an *accessorie* in the sense of an 'appendage' or 'annex', but rather, as Zellweger demonstrates, it is an *integrating component* of the further evolution of the specific cultural apparatus of *homo ipsi faber*, whose course of design and development is now determined to a great extent socio-politically and no longer exclusively biologically-naturally. **PM**

3. Sigmund Freud ‚Das Unbehagen in der Kultur', in *Das Unbehagen in der Kultur und andere kulturtheoretische Schriften.* Fischer, 2001, pp.29-108.

[OR–000] Relic Rosé pendant, 2006. Mixed media, flock, silver

Gehlens Prothesenlehre geht über diese Tradition hinaus. Für ihn bilden und repräsentieren Prothesen das Geschaffene, Künstliche und Verfügbare schlechthin, das dem Natürlichen als Gesamtheit allen Nicht-Künstlichen und Nicht-Verfügbaren gegenübersteht. ‚Kultur' selbst avanciert so bei Gehlen gleichsam zu einer Prothese, einer künstlichen Natur zweiter Ordnung. Sie schiebt sich als ein Instrument der Anpassung zwischen das ‚Mängelwesen' Mensch und seine primordiale natürliche Umwelt. Diese zweite künstliche Welt schafft sich der *homo protheticus* in seiner Eigenschaft als geborener ‚Künstler' oder eben Prothesenverfertiger, als der er sich auch als sozialer und politischer Mensch erweist.

Nach diesen weiteren Explikationen des Prothesenbegriffs von Gehlen sollte es nun möglich sein, den prothetischen Status von ‚Schmuck' und damit auch seine besondere Funktionalität als Element von Kultur näher zu bestimmen:

Schmuck nimmt dem Menschen Anpassungsarbeit ab. Schmuckverwendung wirkt kommunikationsentlastend, weichenstellend, setzt filternde Prämissen, sie erleichtert das Eröffnen und Führen der gewünschten, der fruchtbaren Gespräche und Kommunikationsprozesse, sie verhindert die Entstehung unerwünschter Kontakte.

Schmuck beeinflusst somit das Selbstverhältnis ebenso wie das Fremdverhältnis, die Kommunikation mit anderen. Er bewirkt zuweilen auch Selbstmanipulation und die Manipulation Dritter. Im 21. Jahrhundert, so erweitert Zellweger den Begriff, entfaltet die Prothese Schmuckwirkung auch und vielfach besonders dann, wenn sie verdeckt getragen wird, also am, oder gar innerhalb des Körpers. Der Körper selbst wird nun zur gestaltbaren Sache; zu Schmuck.

Schmuck im herkömmlichen Verständnis lässt damit, wie die gesamte menschliche Prothesenproduktion, das Stadium der Organverstärkung und Organakzentuierung allmählich hinter sich. Schmuck ist, wie Zellweger demonstriert, nicht mehr eine *accessio* bzw. ein *accessorie* im Sinne eines ‚Anhängsels' oder ‚Anbaus', sondern ein integrierender Bestandteil der zur weiteren Evolution bestimmten kulturellen Apparatur des *homo ipsi faber*, deren Gestaltung und Entwicklung weitgehend sozio-politisch und nicht mehr ausschliesslich biologisch-natürlich determiniert verläuft.

Dr. Pietro Morandi
Dozent an der HgkZ, Hochschule der Künste Zürich, Institut for Cultural Studies in Arts, Media and Design; Privatdozent im Lehrbereich Politische Theorie der Universität Potsdam

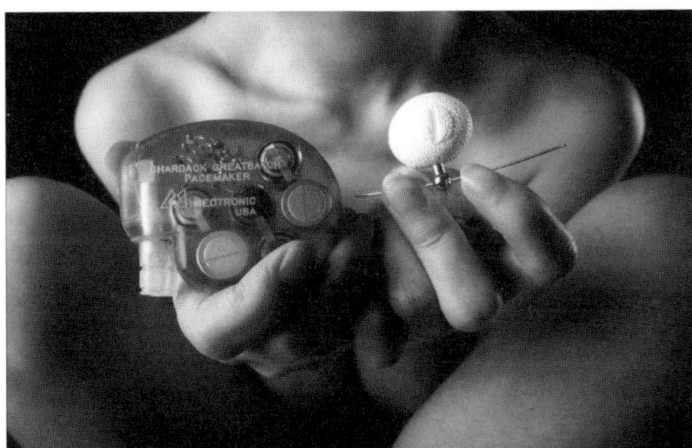

Pacemaker and **Body Piece Switch Q**, 1996

[FF-1] Brooch, 1990. Found object, bone, steel pin. h=155 mm

[FF-1]

[FF-2]

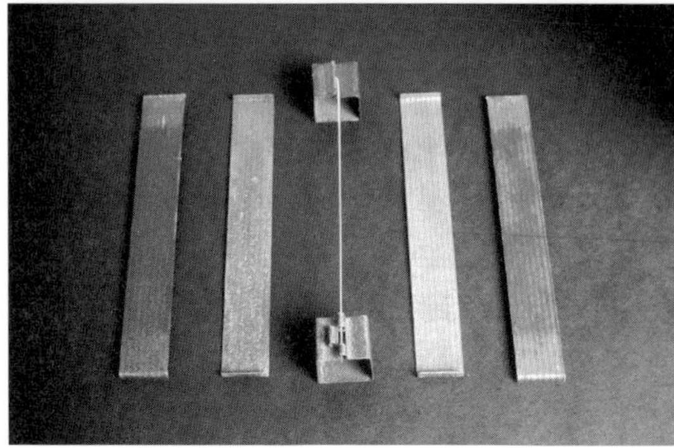

Industrial waste, iron

FF—90.94—M[60-67]

Finds and Fakes

Found industrial materials and natural objects become symbols and signs. How to define 'natural' and 'authentic' in an increasingly urbanised landscape, a man-made natural world?

[FF–2] Brigitte wearing her ring, 1994. Steel, ceramic shell casting. 55 x 68 mm

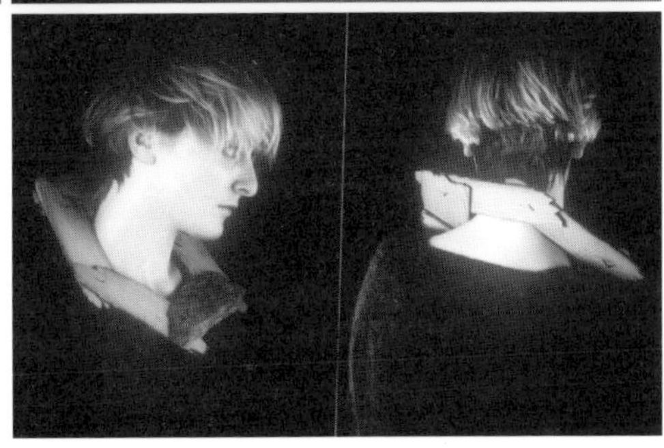

These objects with their sculptural dimensions are to be placed above or in the hollow of the hand. They juxtapose materials of different origins and found objects used as they are. Zellweger seeks to redefine human perception of – and communication with – jewellery; the way people are transformed by objects or vice versa, as well as their influence on the environment and nature and their place in history." SYLVIE LAMBERT, 1998

[FF–6] Double pendant, 1992. Found objects, iron. h=220 mm

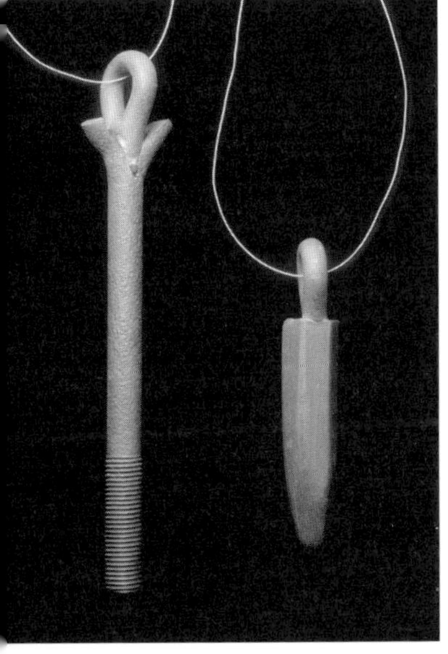

[FF–5] Ring, 1992. Found objects, iron tools, bone. 70 x 150 x 50 mm. Angermuseum Collection, Erfurt

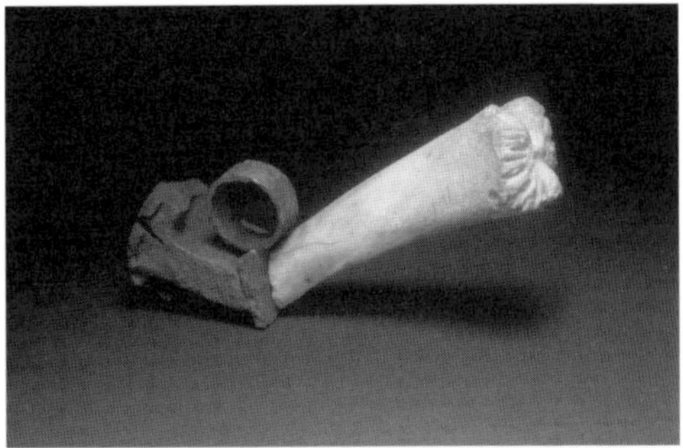

[FF–7] Fork-ring, 1992. Found objects, iron. Angermuseum Collection, Erfurt

[FF-8]

Industrial ceramic shell cast

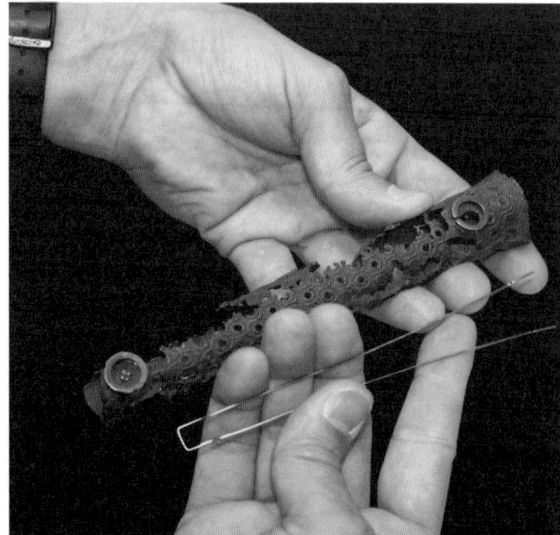

[FF-9] Brooch, 1993. Steel, detachable steel pin. Private Collection

FF-90.94-S[60-67]

[FF-8] Brooches, 1993-1994. Steel, ceramic shell casting. h=170 mm

[FF–10] Brooch, 1994. Steel, ceramic shell casting. 130 mm

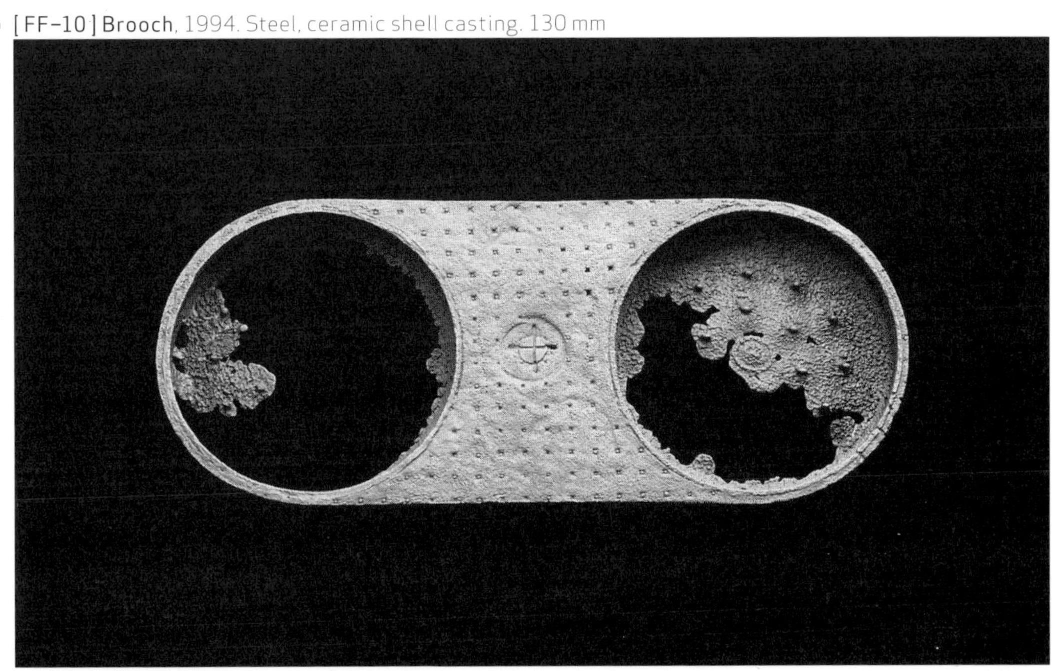

[FF–11] Brooches, 1993. Steel, ceramic shell casting. Ø 65 mm

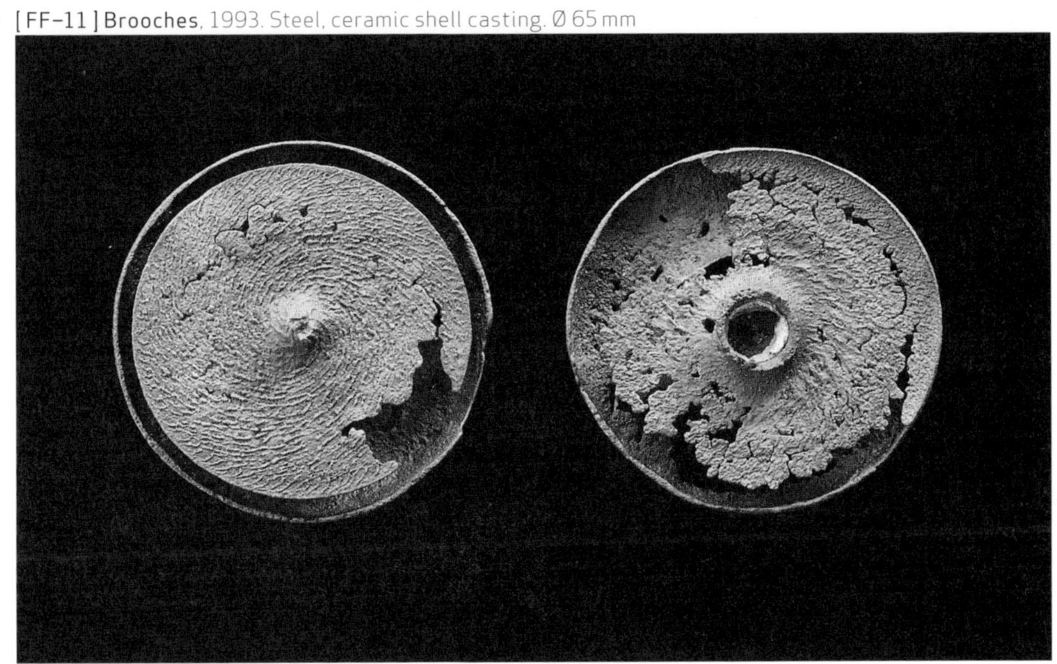

[CH–1] Chain, 1995. Steel, latex. L=270 cm. Crafts Council Collection, London

[CH-1]

Fusako wearing **Chain**, 1995

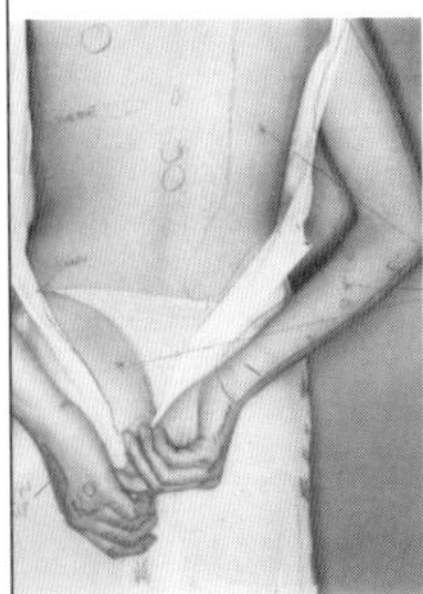

Portraying
the (perfect)
body: retouch
indications for
fashion magazine

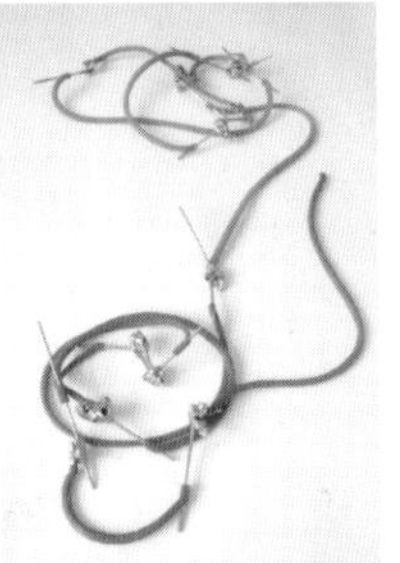

[CH–2] Red Chain,
1995

[CH–1]

Chains

"In *Chains*, the symbolic imagery of technology and nature are joined together as life-giving forces, while the structure of the materials, latex and mild steel, give an illusion of decomposing". RALPH TURNER, 1996

[CH–2] Red Chain, 1995. Steel, latex. L=270 cm. MIMA, Institute of Modern Art Collection, Middlesborough

Installing honey combs, bees ⊢————————⊣

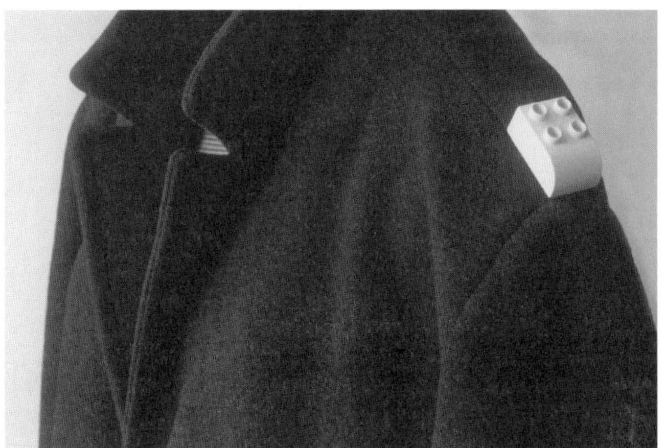

[LW–2] Brooch for a 4-star general, 1993. Gold 22ct

LW–93–S[71-73]

Lego Works

Billboard installation in the city of Graz (A), *Kunst auf Zeit*, 1993. Zellweger dealt with environmental issues and reflected upon the tight interdependence between nature and artifice. Bees were buzzing around an image of an over-sized Lego brick, whose cell-like structure recalls that of the honeycomb. Shown partly filled with oil, the Lego piece refers to the man-made impurity one finds in nature today. The installation was awarded a prize by the Department of Culture of Graz.

[LW–1] Untitled, Billboard- installation Graz, 1993 ⊢————

as heller Freude.

der
ERZÄHLKUNST

Low-tech electroforming unit

Adaptation of industrial process to work in small studio environment: Raw Polystyrene consists of tiny gas filled beads. These beads are expanded in two stages with the help of steam and pressure. Industry uses aluminium moulds in which the material expands to receive its final shape. In the studio a customised pressure cooker is used to expand the polystyrene in electro-formed copper moulds

Body Pieces

"I became aware of polystyrene for the first time in 1986, where small and larger bits of it floated even in a remote part of the Mekong River. It is a universal waste material, an omnipresent substance, a by-product of commodities today." CZ

Electroformed copper-mould, polystyrene expanded, different densities

Customised pressure cooker to expand polystyrene

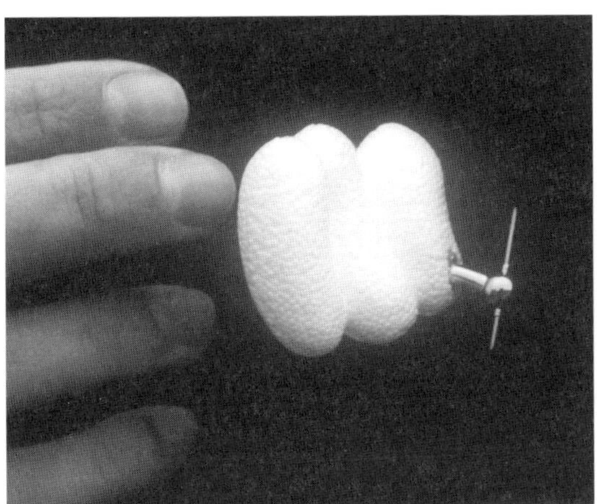

[BP–1] Body Piece Paddy, 1996. Expanded polystyrene, silver chrome-plated, steel

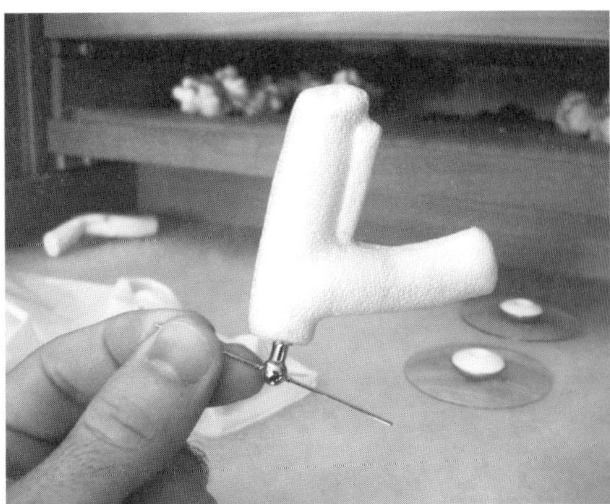

[BP–2] Body Piece BV3, 1996. Expanded polystyrene, silver chrome-plated, steel

 Body Pieces

[BP–3] Body Piece 3B neckpiece, 1997. Expanded polystyrene, silver chrome-plated, silicone tube

[BP-3]

[BP-4]

[BP–5] Body Piece IE4 neckpiece, 1997. Expanded polystyrene, silver chrome-plated, silicone tube. FNAC National Foundation for Contemporary Art Collection, Paris

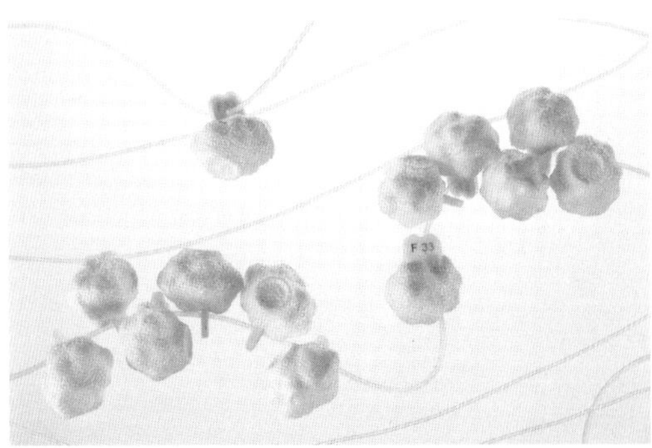

[BP–6] Commodity Chain F33, 1996. Expanded polystyrene, silver chrome-plated, silicone tube, nylon. L= 160 cm

[BP–7] Commodity Chain K22, 1997. Expanded polystyrene, silver chrome-plated, silicone tube, nylon. L= 160 cm

BP–96.03–L[74-83] Commodity Chain

[BP–4] Elizabeth holding Body Piece 3Q, 1997. Expanded polystyrene

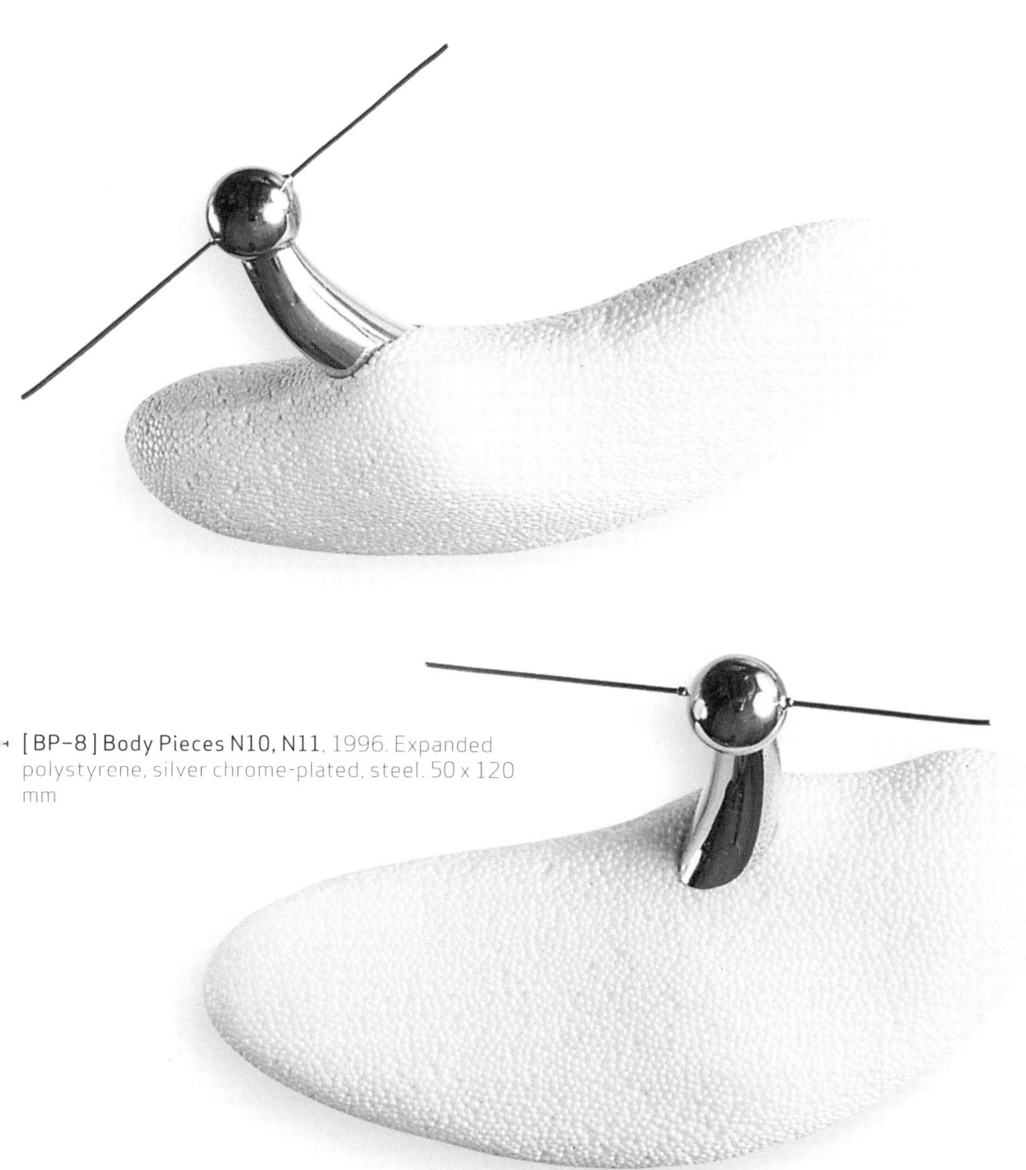

"The artefacts I produce can be seen as made *for* the body; as well as they are also artefacts *about* the body. *Body Pieces* are prostheses with a mental dimension, they are made of a disposable material like polystyrene, related to consumer society. In our collective search for improvement, ultimate functionality, beauty and perfection, the body itself has also been commodified, it has become a luxury item." CZ

[BP–7] Cristina wearing **Commodity Chain K22**, 1997

[BP-7]

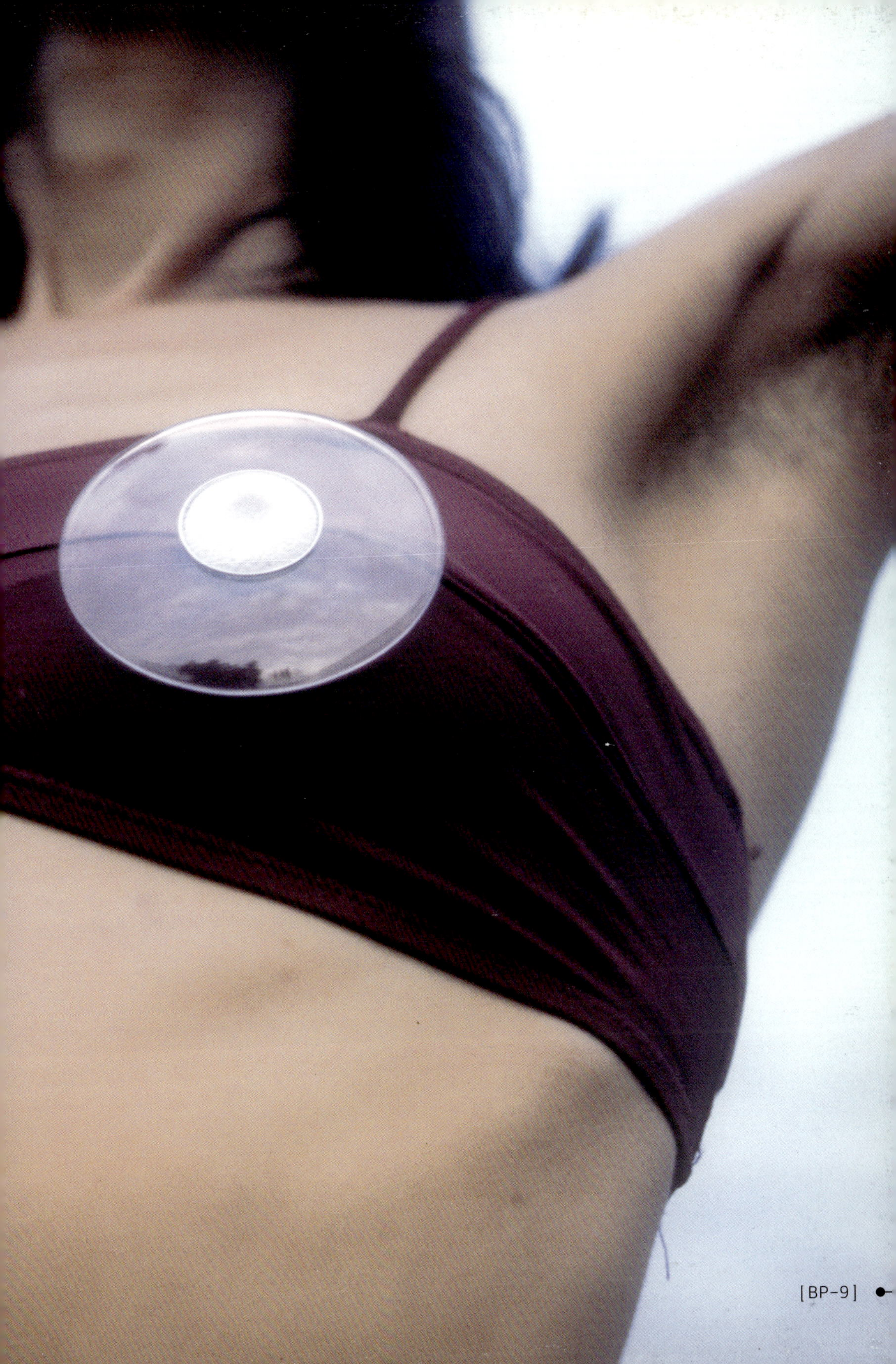

[BP-9]

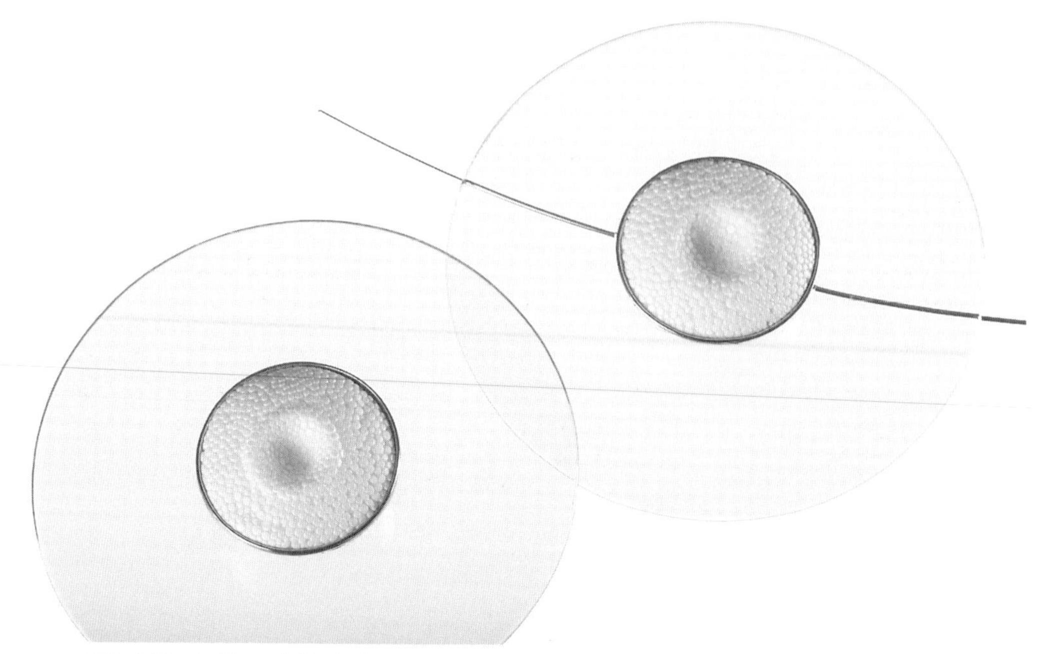

[BP–9] Body Piece E, Body Piece EE, 1997.
Glass, expanded polystyrene, silver chrome-plated, stainless steel pin

[BP–10] Body Pieces GNY, 1997-1998. Expanded polystyrene,
velcro. Ø50mm

Subverting the conventional dialectic between material and meaning, polystyrene
becomes precious in order to embody fragility and emotion.

BP–96.03–L[74-83]

[BP–9] Body Piece E, 1997

[BP–11] **Window Shopping**, Installation, 2003. Project **Kultur im Kasten**, Wädenswil, Switzerland. Mirrors 90°, polystyrene Body Pieces, graphic elements

The intervention Window Shopping confronts the public passing a subway. Attracted by two mirrors in the centre of an otherwise empty showcase people stop. On close inspection, one to two polystyrene Body Pieces in the shape of nipples appear and disappear. Like in a mirage, the viewer sees the objects as if they were placed on his/her own body. Window Shopping poses questions concerning body conformity and the illusory body in advertising.

BP–96.03–L[74-83]   Window Shopping

[DJ–1] **Data Jewel** air-box packaging, 1999. Stainless steel gold-plated, silver chain

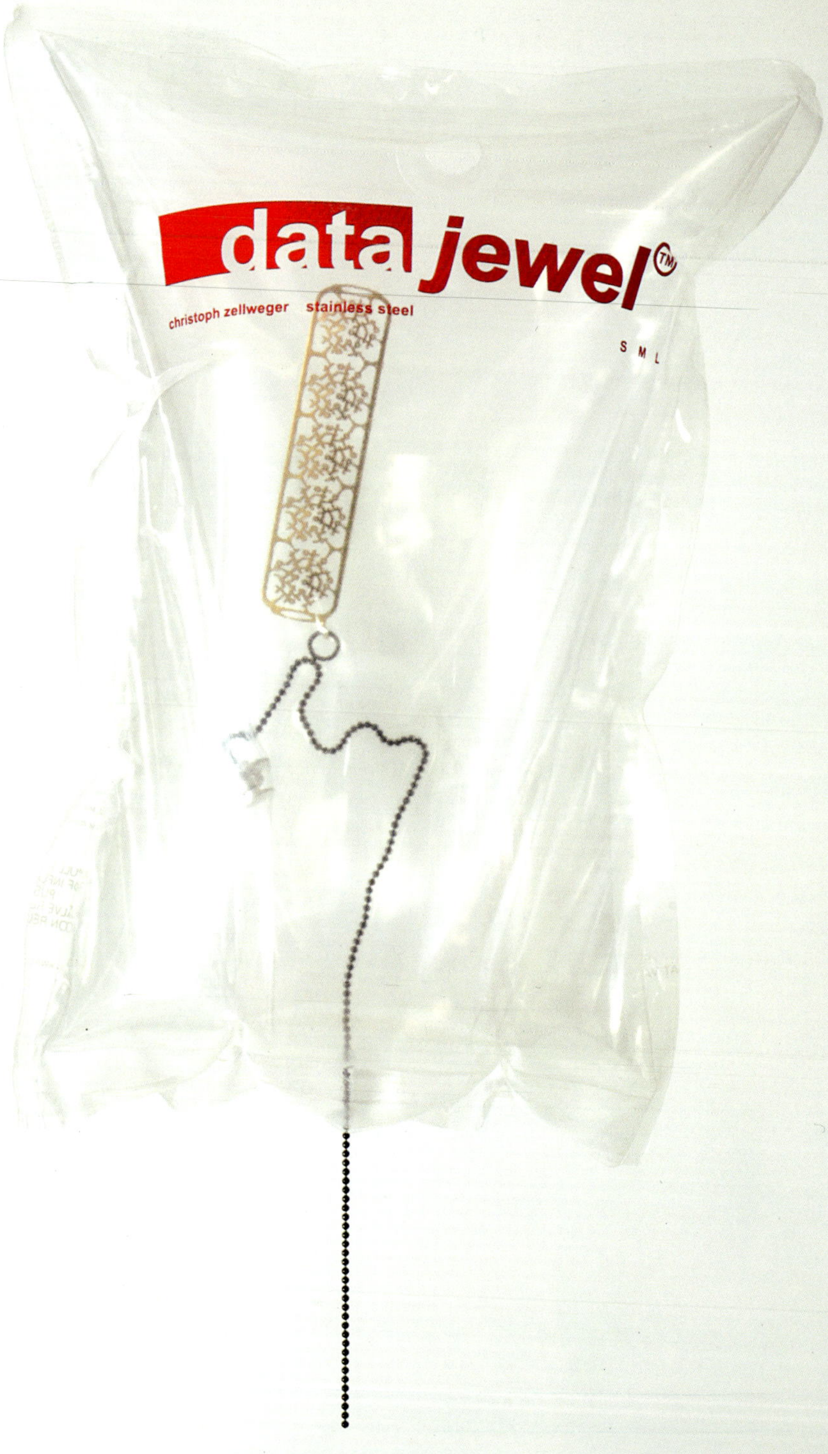

data jewel ™
christoph zellweger   stainless steel
S M L

[DJ-2]

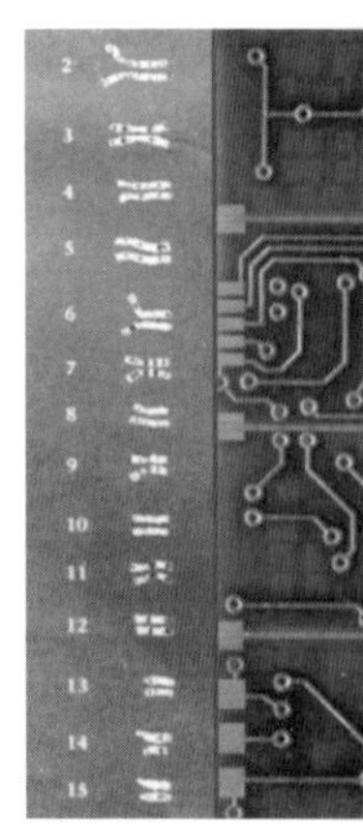

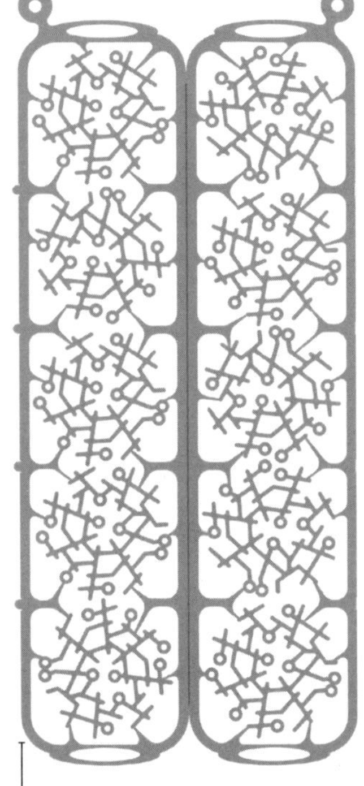

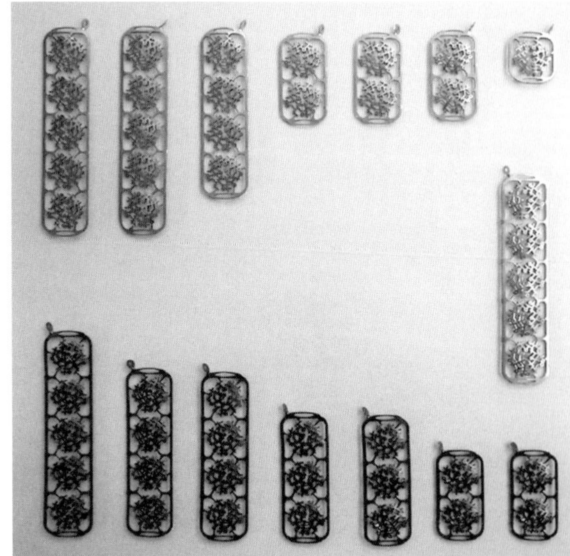

Data Jewels

Data Jewels

Whether arabesque or code of arms, microchip or genetic fingerprint or tattoo, ornament serves as the carrier of information. Designed on the computer, *Data Jewels* relate to the tradition of jewellery as a medium for communicating identity, beliefs, social status and taste. The minute, shiny patterns recall the sense of preciousness and delicacy of classic jewellery while the technological aesthetic suggests newer strategies of encoding meaning.

[DJ−2] **Data Jewel** chain, 2006. Stainless steel gold-plated, silver

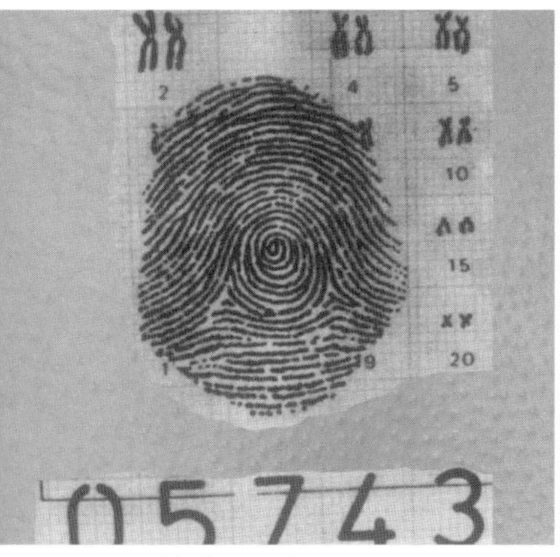

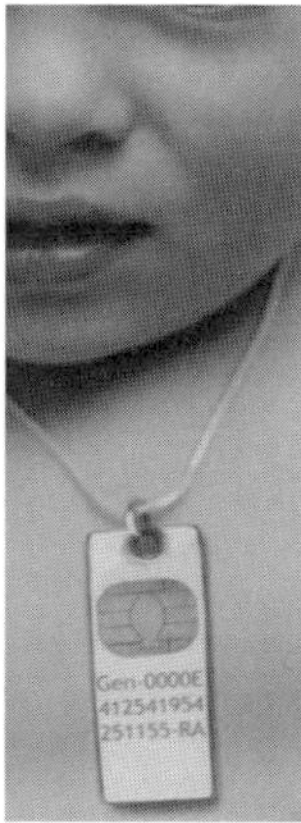

rnament and information

Image: Der Spiegel

[DJ–3] Ornament and banality. Beatriz wearing
unny Banal pendant, 2001

[DJ–4] Freya showing off her **Data Jewel**

[DJ–5] Koichiro wearing **Data Jewel**, 2001. Stainless steel

[DJ-5]

[DJ-6] ●

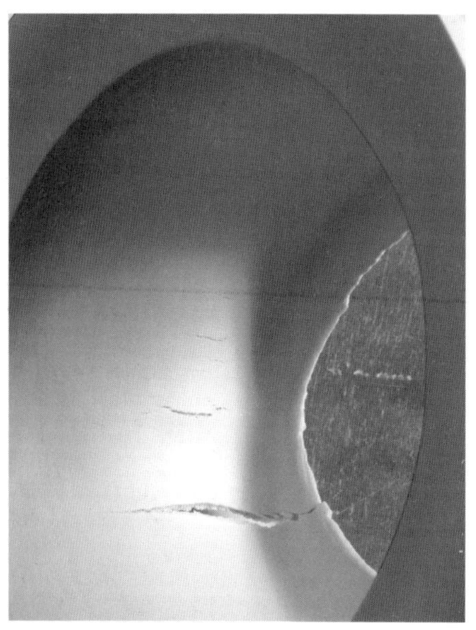

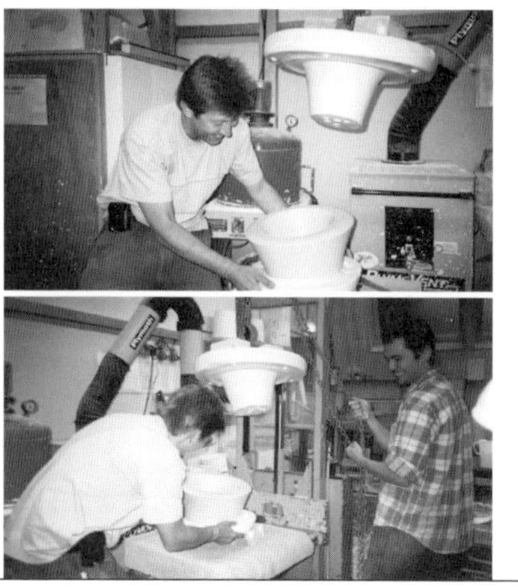

[PW-2] **Untitled**, 2001. Porcelain and earthenware. Ø 31 cm. Double-skinned objects designed to distort and break during firing

Porcelain Works

Porcelain is a material not dissimilar to the substance bones are created from. A three month working period as artist-in-residence at the European Ceramic Work Centre (EKWC) in Hertogenbosch (NL) lead to a body of work concerned with vulnerability which made reference to bones, genes and seeds. The results were shown at the exhibition *Slip - Artists in the Netherlands and in England Working with Ceramics*, Sainsbury Centre for Visual Arts, Norwich (UK) and Frans Hals Museum, Haarlem (NL), 2002.

[DJ-6] **Seeds** neckpiece, 2006. Stainless steel gold-plated, silver

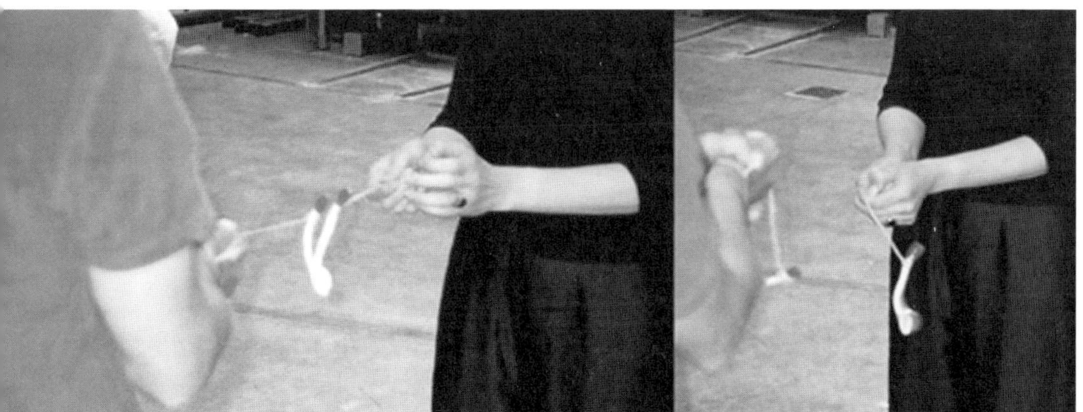

[PW–3] Pulled, 2001

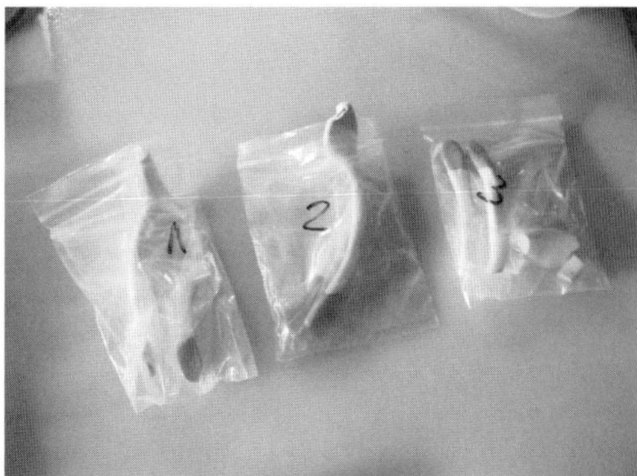

Relics of **Pulled** performance.
Fragments of belief

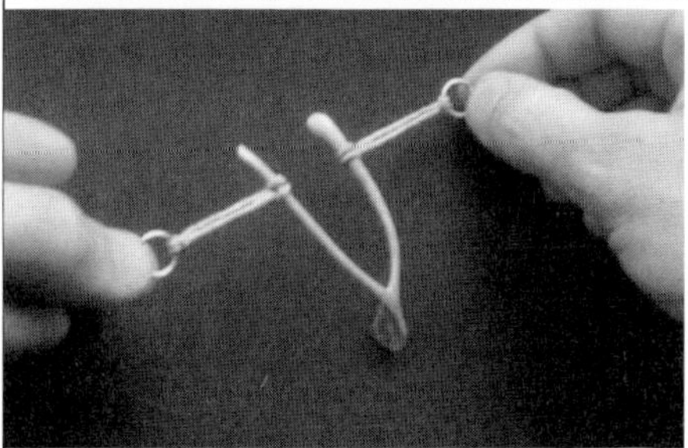

Make a wish, pull… At some point, a porcelain wishbone also breaks. Somebody
wins and for a short moment the belief in believing is lost… Thinking about the
'right faith', the performance of pulling three wishbones took place on the 31st of
August in 2001 at the European Ceramic Work Centre several days after a major
escalation in Ramallah.

PW–01–M[90-93]   *Pulled*

[PW-4] Untitled, 2001. Porcelain

[PW-4]

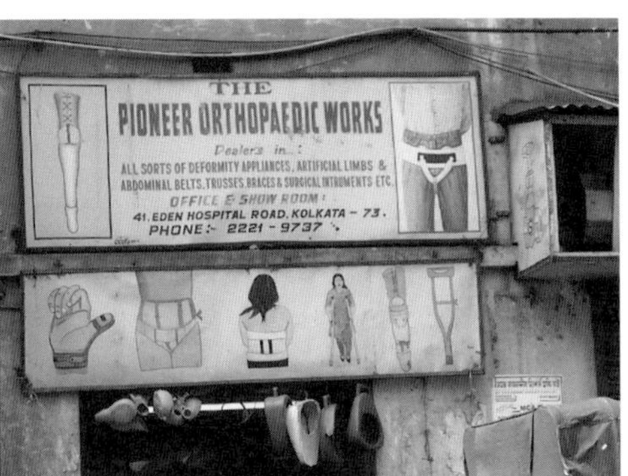

India 2006. Billboard advertising

England 2006. Man with artificial ear

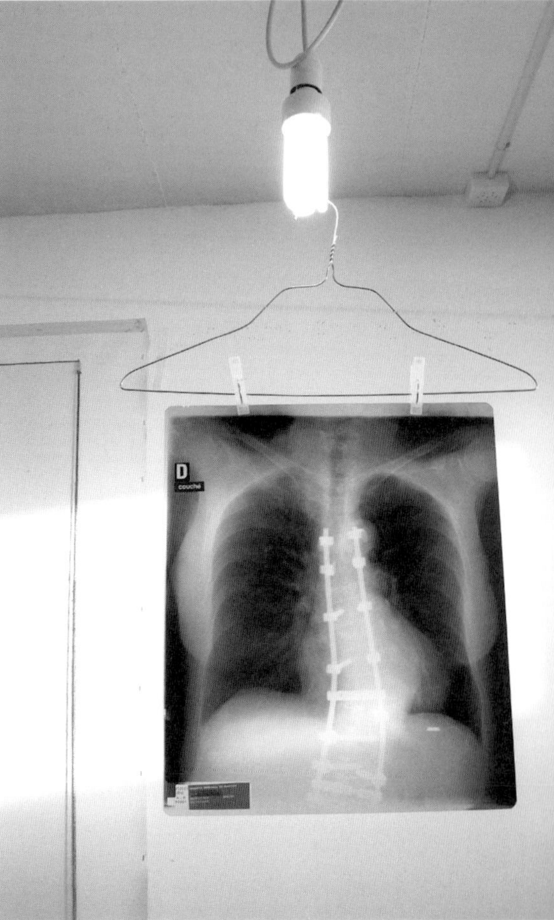

X-ray, spine of Monique, 1998

Foreign Bodies

More and more highly refined objects are being inserted as implants into the interior of the body for medical or aesthetic reasons. Foreign Bodies reflect on this development. Although visually referring to implants, they are worn on the surface of the skin, traditionally, as adornments. Wearing a piece that resembles a prosthesis is a transgression, subverting once more the borders between the interior and exterior of the body. Foreign Bodies offer a hallucinatory view on the relationship between the subject and its objects by revealing things that are intended to remain hidden. Contradictory feelings of wonder and estrangement merge as the body becomes transparent and opposites fuse into one single aesthetic experience.

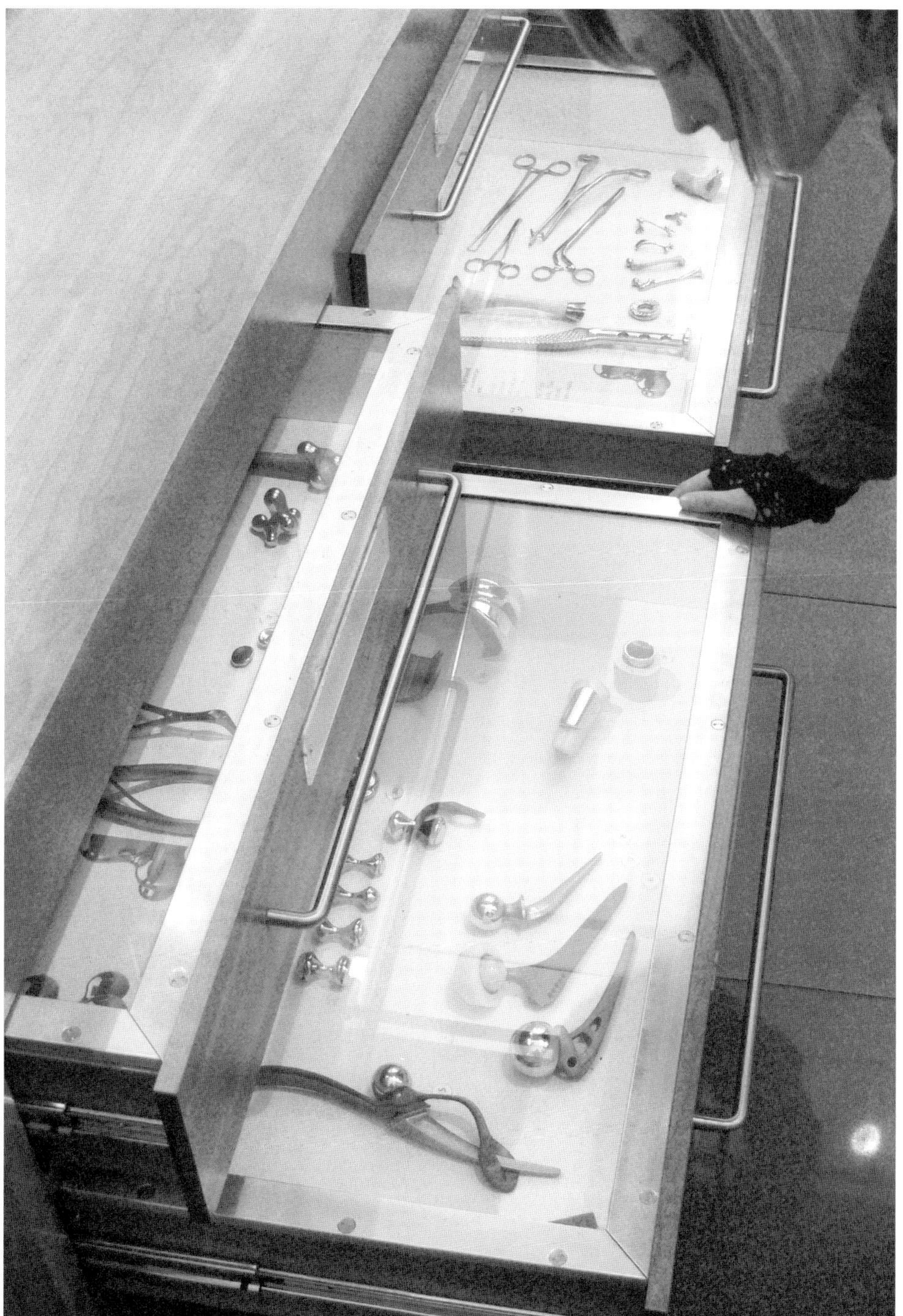

[FB–1] Medical Grade 316, intervention, Metalwork Gallery/ Millennium Gallery 2006.
Twenty-three Foreign Body pieces, produced in bio- compatible Medical Grade 316 steel, were
displayed alongside commercial orthopedic components of the same material. The intervention
reflected on the definition of metalwork today. It shifted the concept of preciousness and luxury
towards a debate on medical science and body design

[FB–2] Hip Piece #2401x0, 2002. Second-hand hip replacements, leather. h=500 mm

[FB-2]

[FB-3]

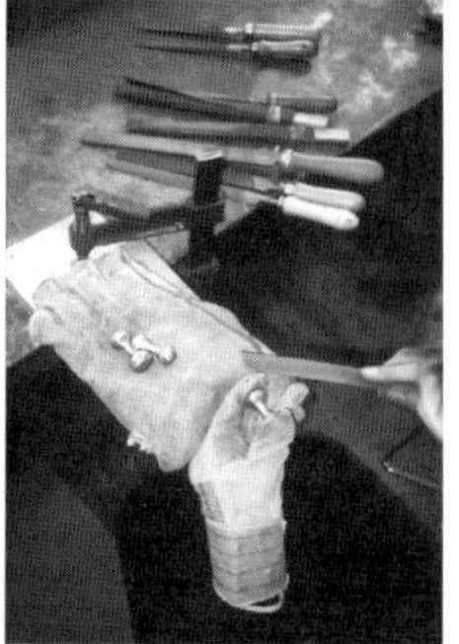

Casting of **Foreign Bodies** and **Fluids** in bio-compatible medical steel. Industrial Ceramic Shell Casting

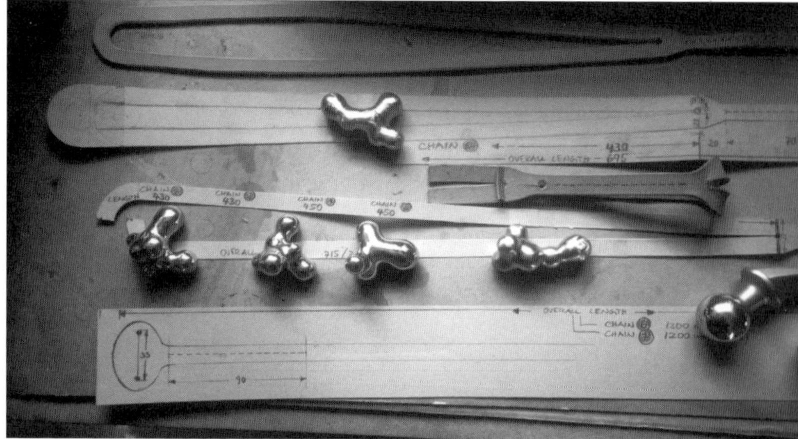

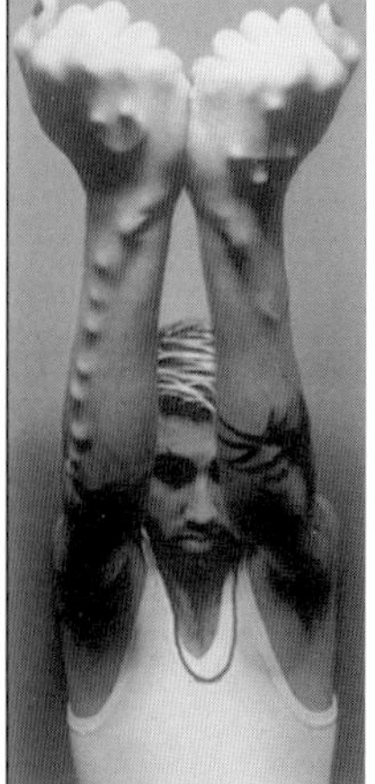

Steve Hayworth with steel implants.
Image: Der Spiegel, 1998

[FB–3] Fluids, 2002. Medical steel, leather. 45 x 45 x 50 mm

The painstaking and perfect execution of *Fluids* doesn't allow the viewer to notice any trace of the maker's hand. Sensual, highly polished medical steel objects with a perceptible industrial finish set up interesting and disturbing parallels between body organs and luxury items.

FB—00.05—XL[94-105] Fluids

[FB–3] Monique wearing **Hip Piece**, 2002

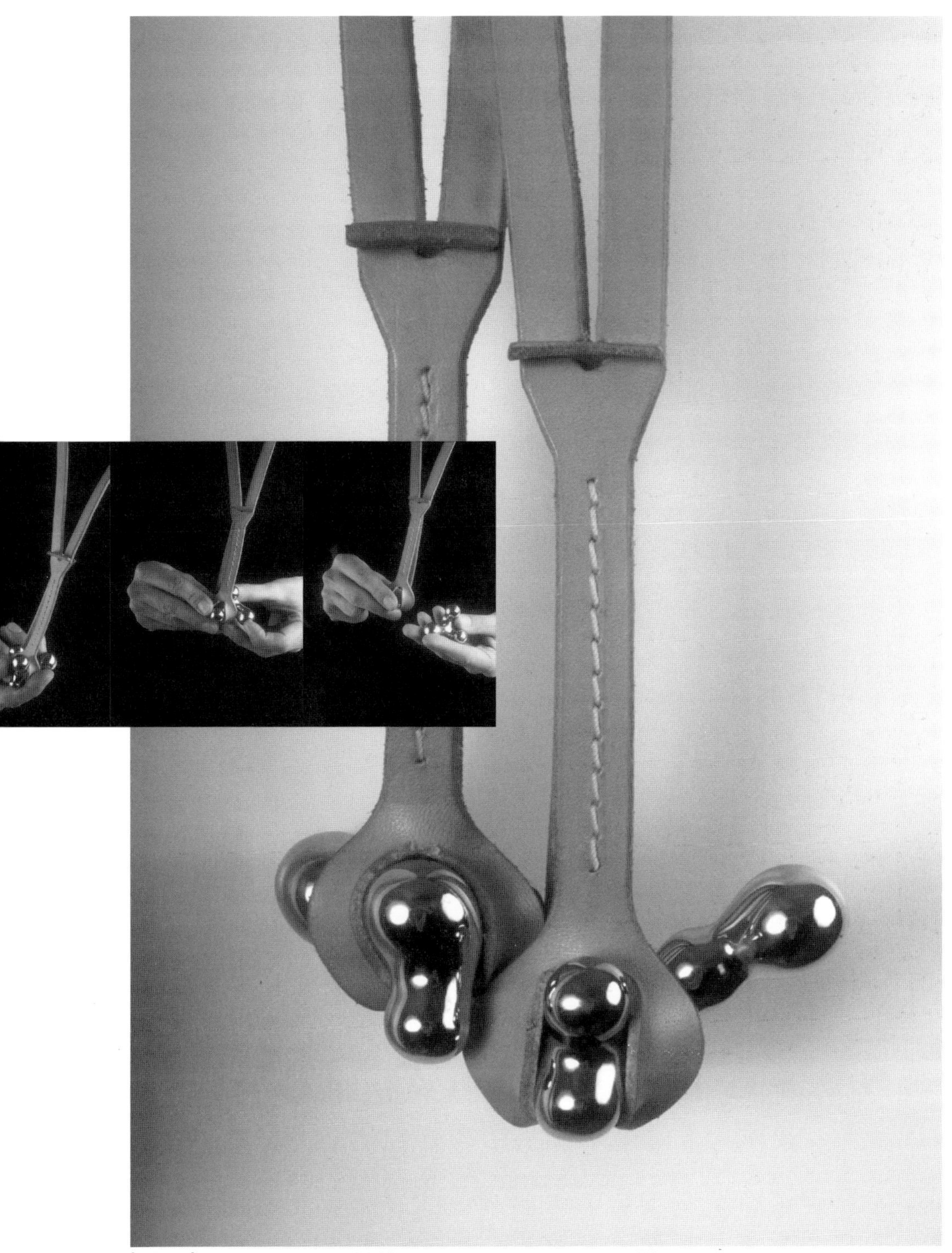

[FB–4] **Fluid** neckpieces, 2002. Medical steel, leather. h= 450 mm

[FB–5] **Fremd-Körper** intervention, Swiss National Museum, Zürich, 2005

[FB-5]

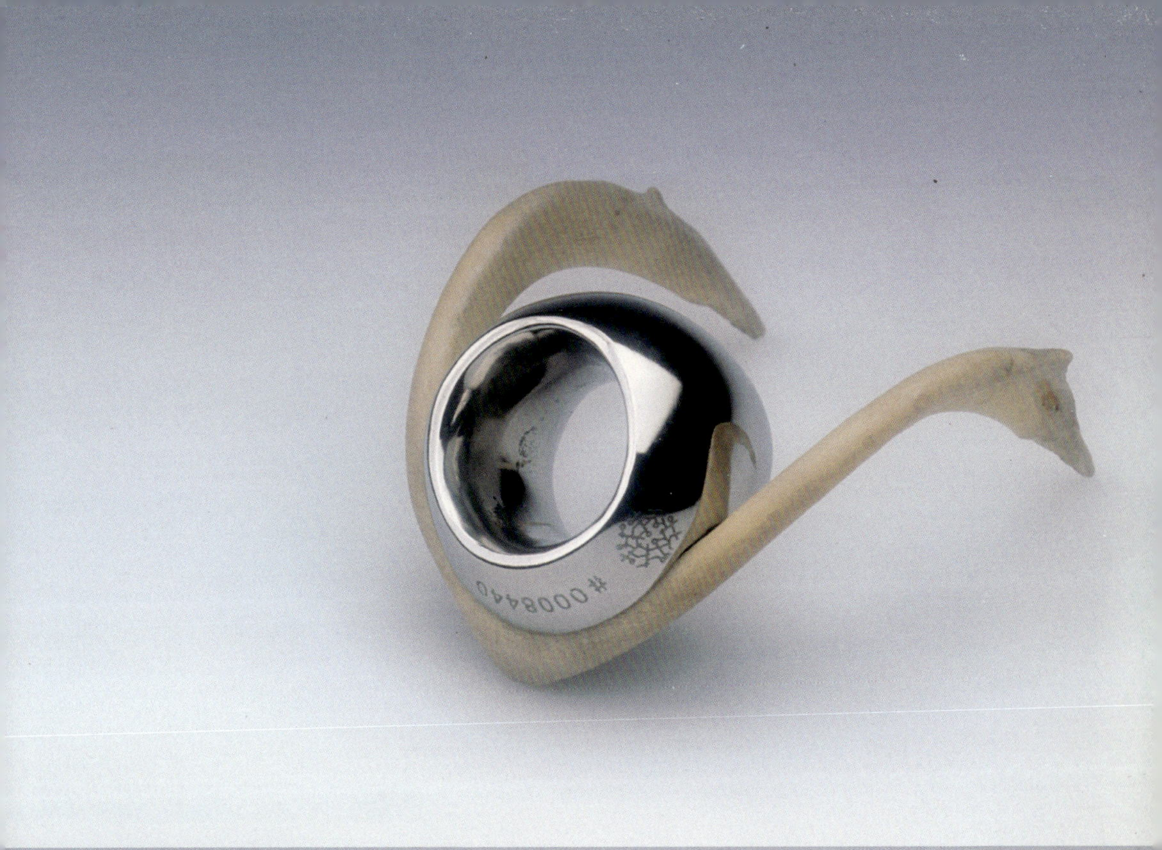

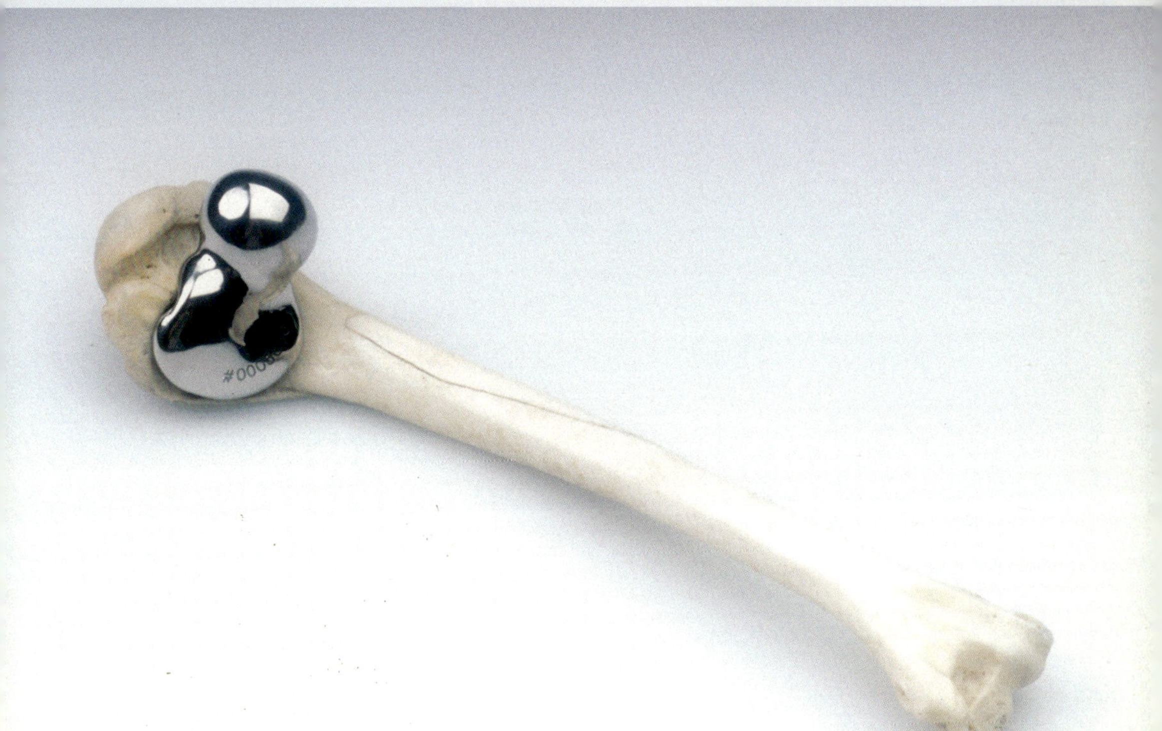

[FB-5] **Fremd-Körper** intervention, Swiss National Museum, Zürich, 2005.
The intervention referred to 'fossiles from the future', imaginary implantable jewellery that
enhanced the ambiguity between the autonomous contemporary art object and the applied,
historical artefact. The work was shown as an additional layer on top of a permanent display of
the archeological museums collection.

FB—00.05—XL[94-105]

[FB-6] **Foreign Body #0008440**, 2003. Medical steel, bone
[FB-7] **Foreign Body #0008130**, 2003. Medical steel, bone

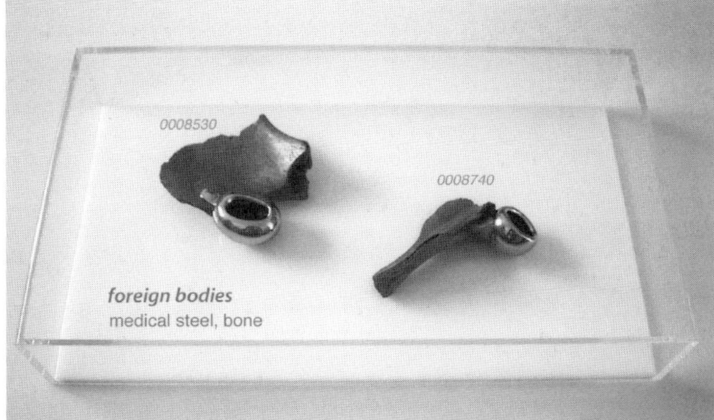

[FB–8] Foreign Bodies #0008530 and #0008220, 2003.
Medical steel, bone. Private Collection

"The idea of being asked to transform a medical implant that has been worn internally for many years into a piece of externally worn jewellery has been an initial inspiration for my work. Next to appreciating the high quality and aesthetics of these implants, I recognise their possible significance to the owner, wearer or onlooker."
CZ, 2000

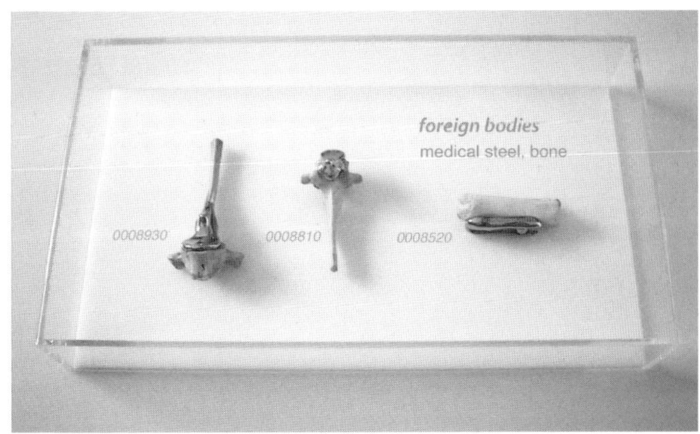

[FB–9] Foreign Bodies #0008930, #0008810 and #0008520, 2003.
Medical steel, bone. Private Collection

[FB–10] Foreign Bodies #0008210, 2003. Medical steel, bone

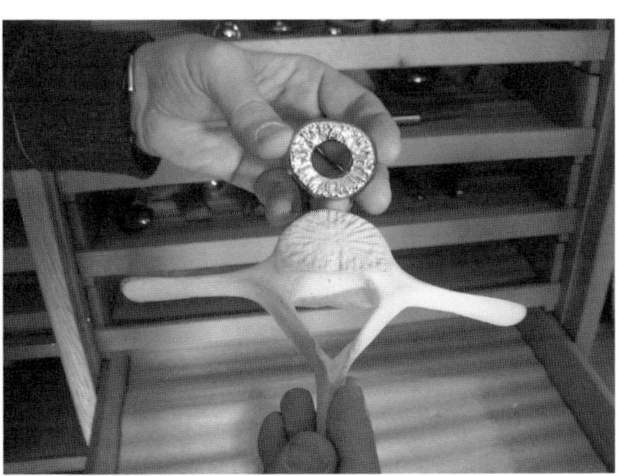

[FB–11] Fremd-Körper display. Galerie Tactile, Geneva, 2003

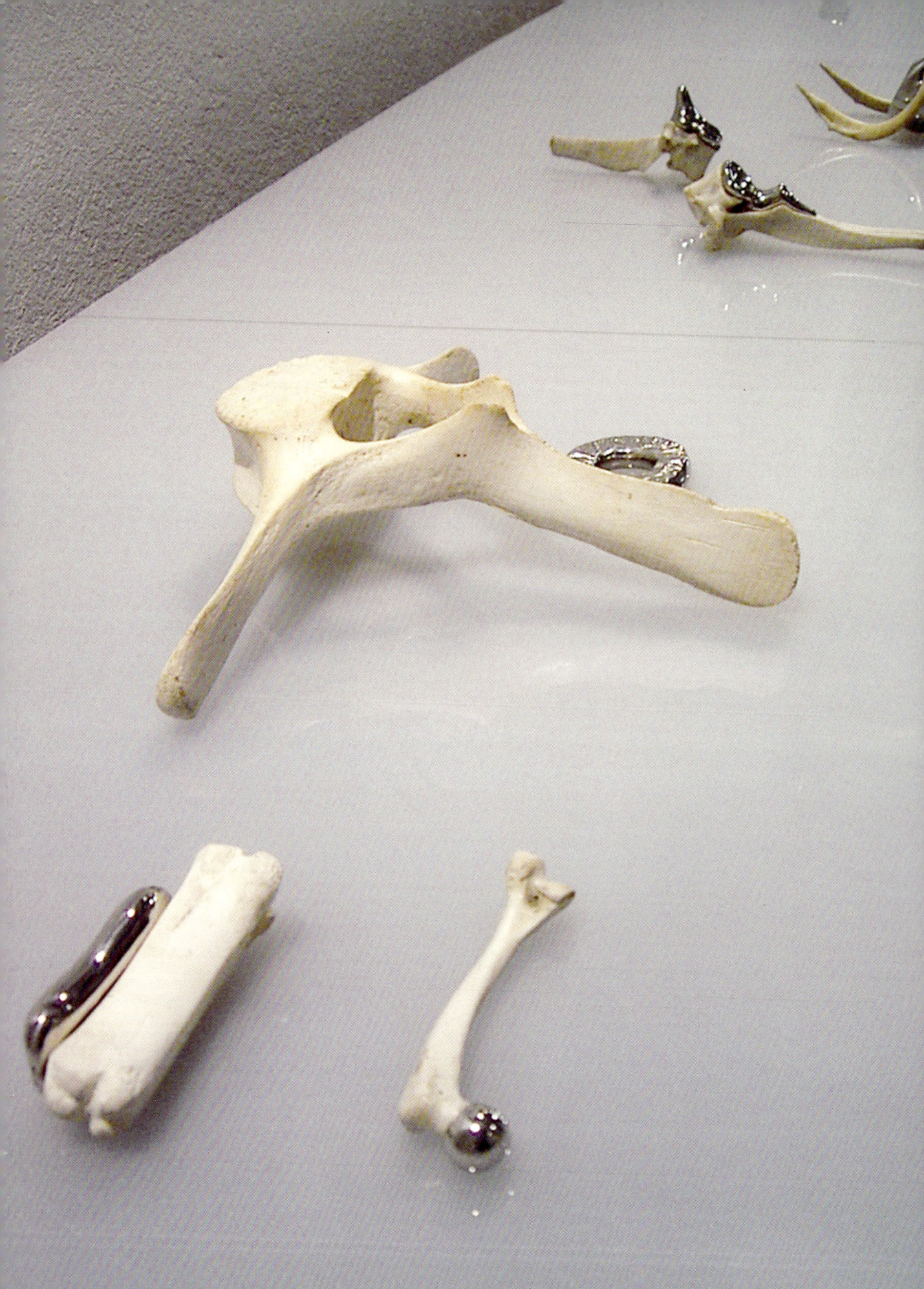

[FB-11]

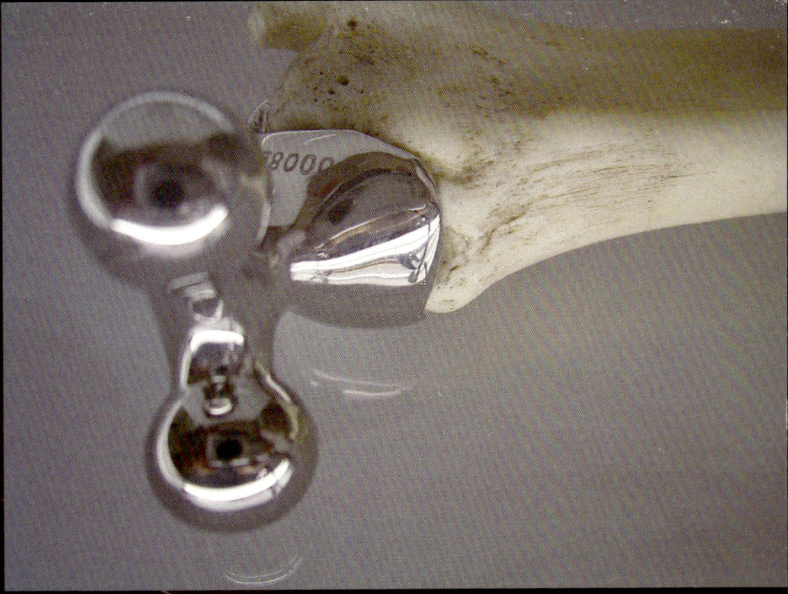

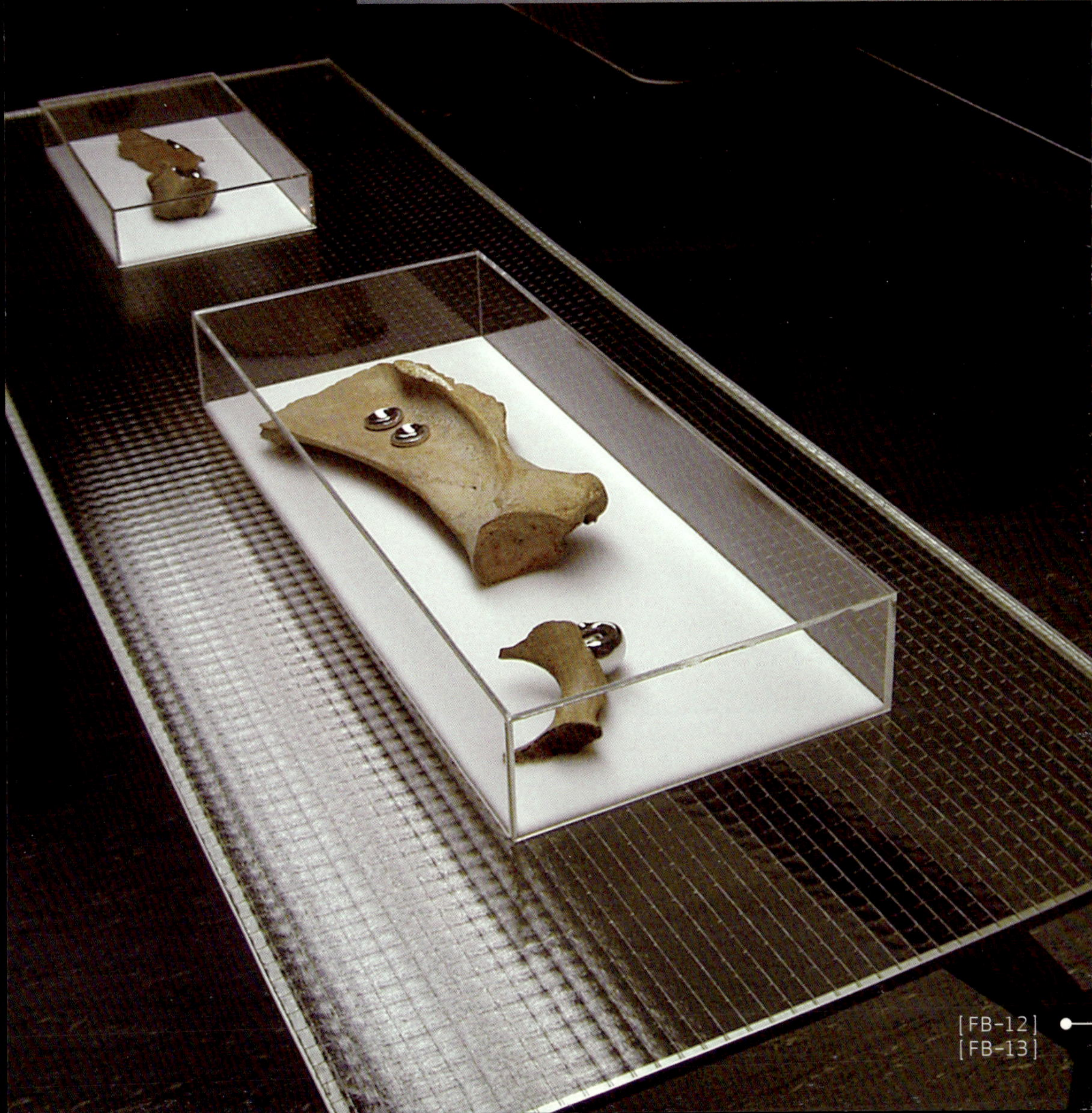

Demolishment of housing units,
ex-tenant. Zurich, 2004.

Knochenarbeit, 2003. Unfired clay bones
on wooden racks, decaying bones

Knochenarbeit

Knochenarbeit (worked-to-the-bone) belongs to the site-specific interventions Zellweger
set up as part of the FUGE Project (Art in Times of Transition), in Zurich, 2003-04. During
one year, a run down social housing estate was offered to artists to use as studio space.
Over one hundred artists worked on site before the demolition. As part of the last public
art-event, Zellweger exposed a large quantity of bones formed out of unfired clay to
the elements - snow and rain. Together with *Places of Dis-belief*, Zellweger's temporary
installations refer to the faith and immigrant histories of the people who had been tenants
of the housing for over forty years. (See also *Pulled*, p.91).

[FB–12] Foreign Bodies #0008120, 2003. Medical steel, bone. (detail)
[FB–13] Fremd-Körper, SchmuckProdukt Zollverein, Essen, 2003

Places of Dis-belief, 2003. Main taps.
Controlling the water, electricity and fuel-supply is part of the fight for the right faith

Pull, 2001. Porcelain wishbones. (see p.91)

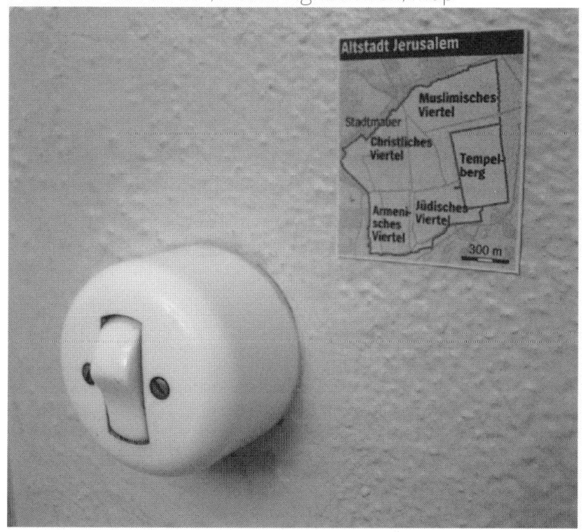

Places of Dis-belief, 2003. Lightswitch, map

[BS–1] Skin, 2006. Natural rubber

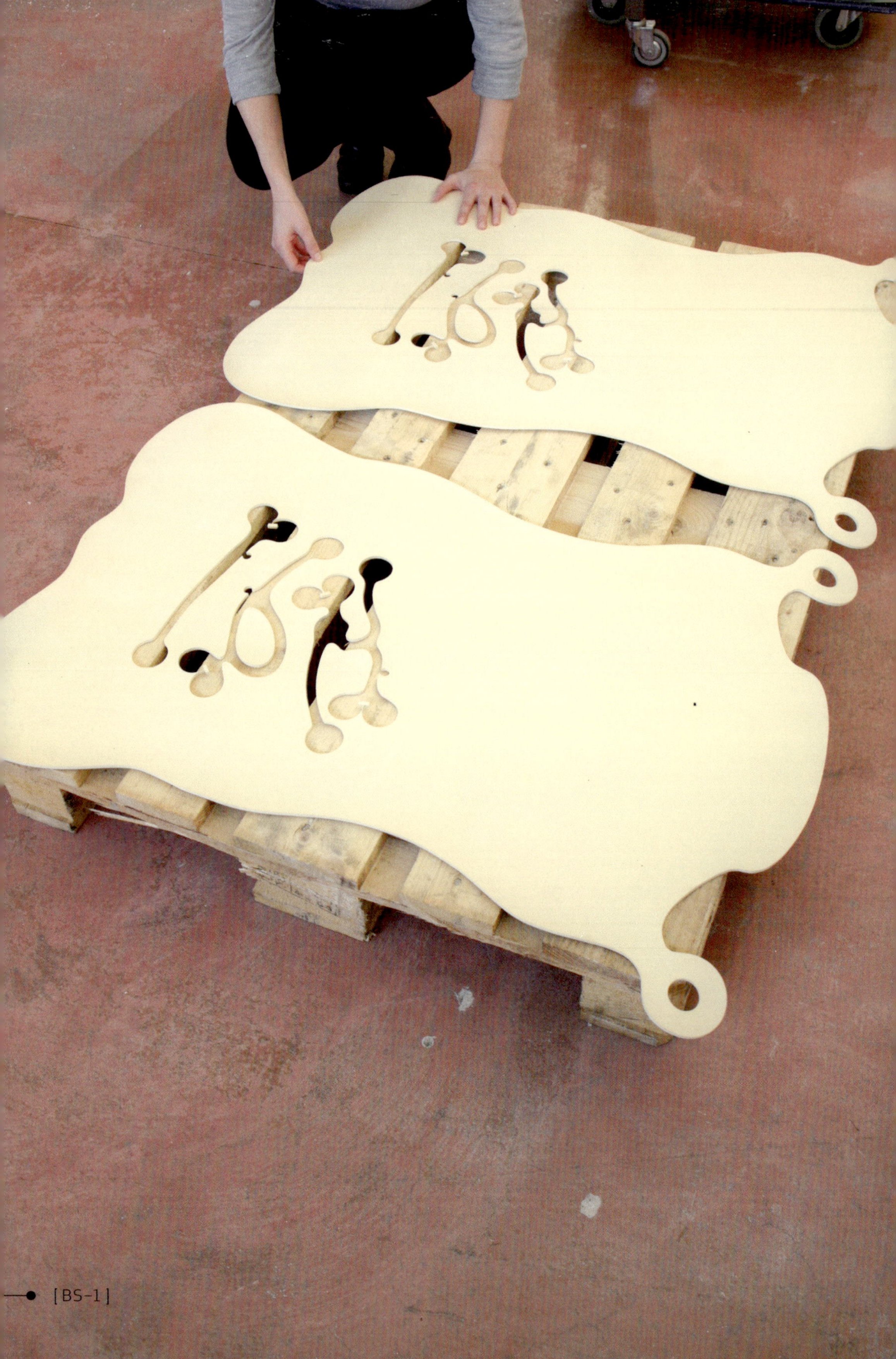

ZELLWEGER

[BS–1] **Skin**, 2006. Natural rubber (detail)

[BS–1] **Skin**, 2006. Natural rubber.
Computer generated drawing

BS–03.07–XL[108-111]

Body Supports

Belts, braces, harnesses and straps are often about supporting, healing and protecting the fragile body. *Body supports*, made out of leather or natural rubber, become emotional prostheses for the contemporary individual.

[BS–2] Body Support, 2006. Natural rubber

[BS–3] Body Support B2, 2004. Steel and leather

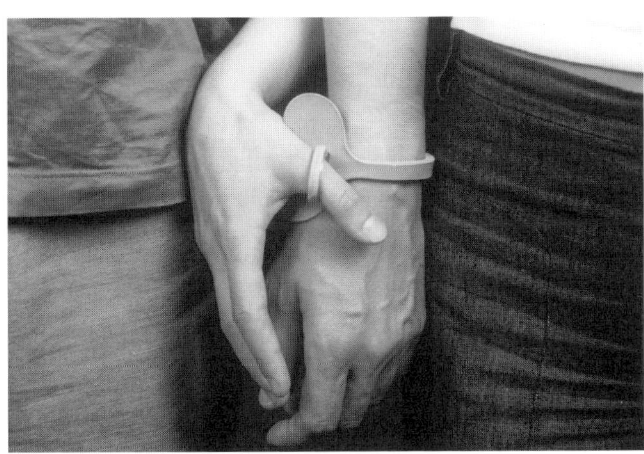

"One could ask whether you should have your nose straightened or fat removed or have your hip joints replaced for prevention... People seem to accept that the body does not have to stay as it is and are willing to invest in improving its functions and cultivating its appearance. Historically this has previously been achieved through the media of body adornment and jewellery. This new development will irreversibly change our view on how we create identity."
CZ, 2001

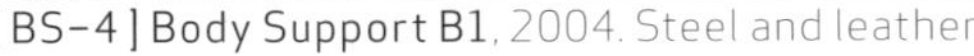

[BS–4] Body Support B1, 2004. Steel and leather

[RH–1] Blanket work, 2004 ⊢———

[RH-1]

[RH-2]

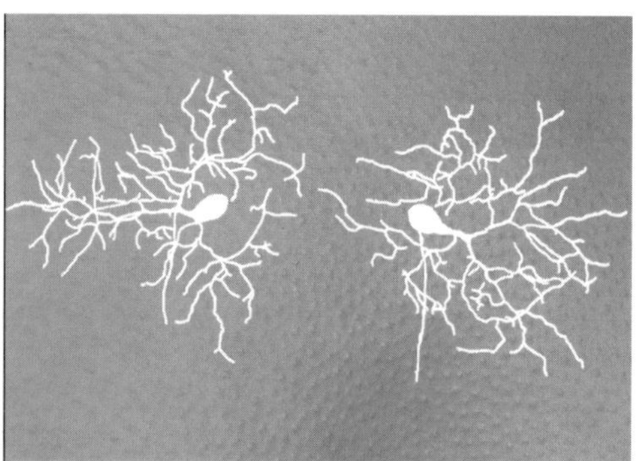

Root-drawing

Rhizome and pattern studies on paper,
leather and textiles, 2002

Lace fabricated in St. Gallen, 2003

Rhizome

A different way of approaching work is needed when one starts with the idea to not
follow the plan, but rather to follow impulse, opportunity and chance. Drawing and
developing patterns become an exercise that takes time, unfocused time, time for
not allowing any one thought to dominate another. *Rhizome* follows the principle of
evolving, like root systems which develop out of a process into a pattern.

[RH−2] Rhizome T-Shirts, 2004

What does one need to escape the limitations inherent in linear thinking? What defines and differentiates natural growth from man-made structures? Do rhizomes provide answers on how to deal with increasing complexity? (see p.144)

Blankets with traditional floral pattern, **Rhizome** cutouts, textile, 2003

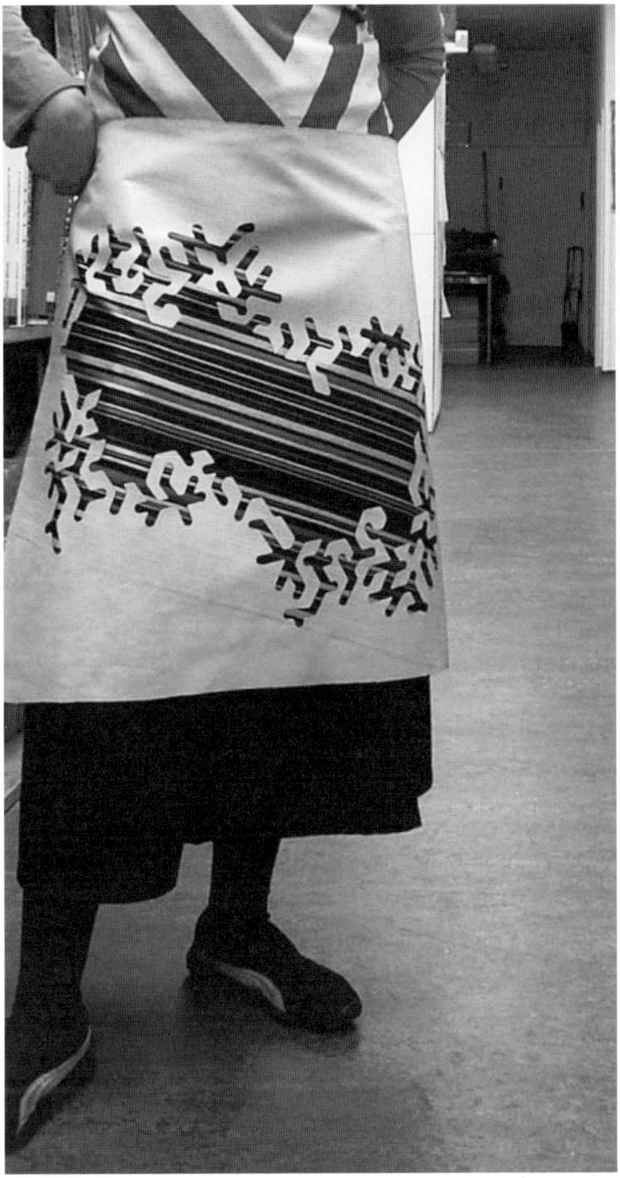

[RH-3] Applying tests at Jakob Schlaepfer, haute-couture and high-tech textile design and manufacturing company, St Gallen (CH)

[RH-4] **Rhizome** wrist-piece, 2006. Natural rubber

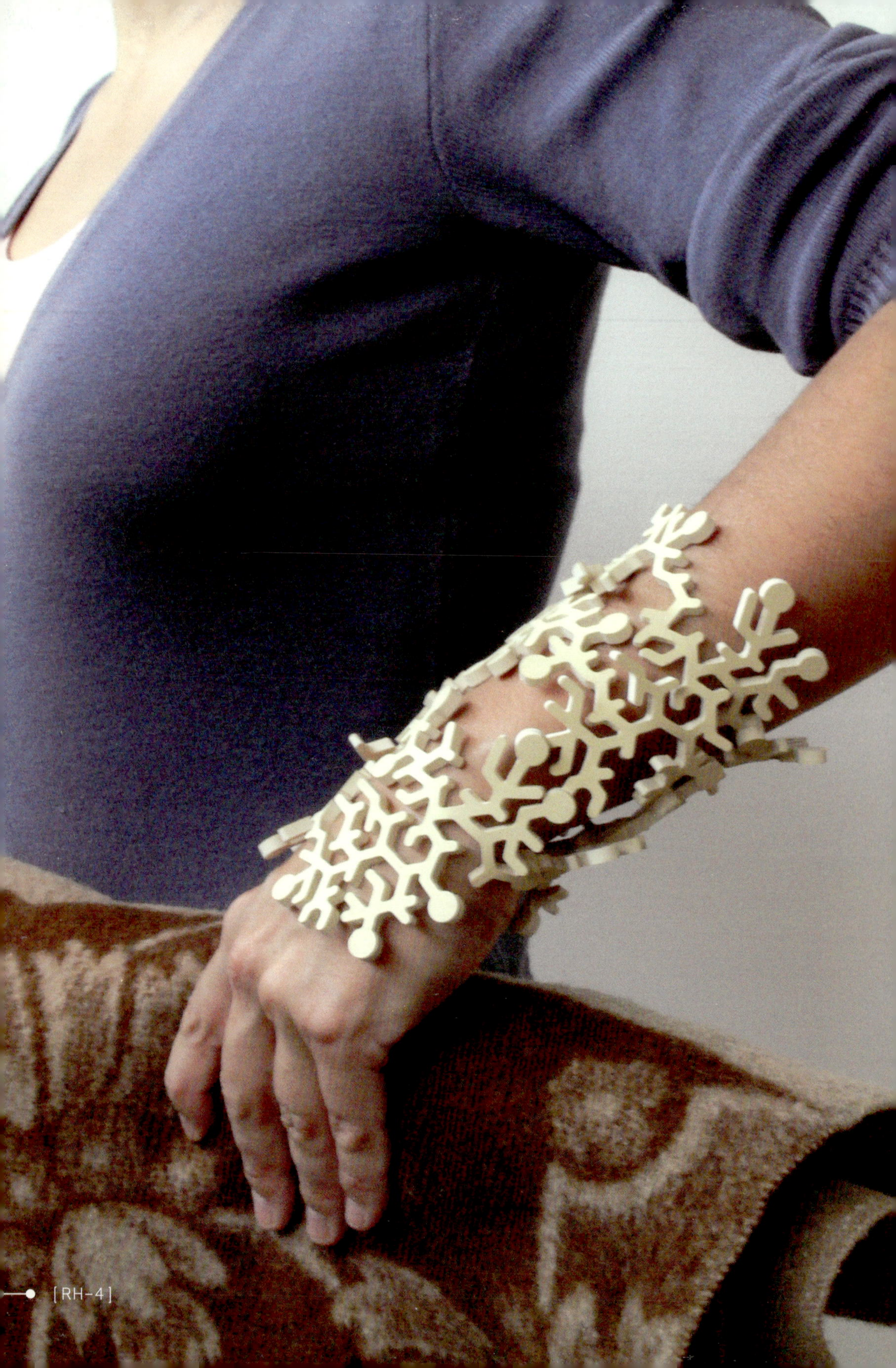

[RH-4]

[RH-4]

Studio view, samples of water-jet
and laser-cuttings, 2006

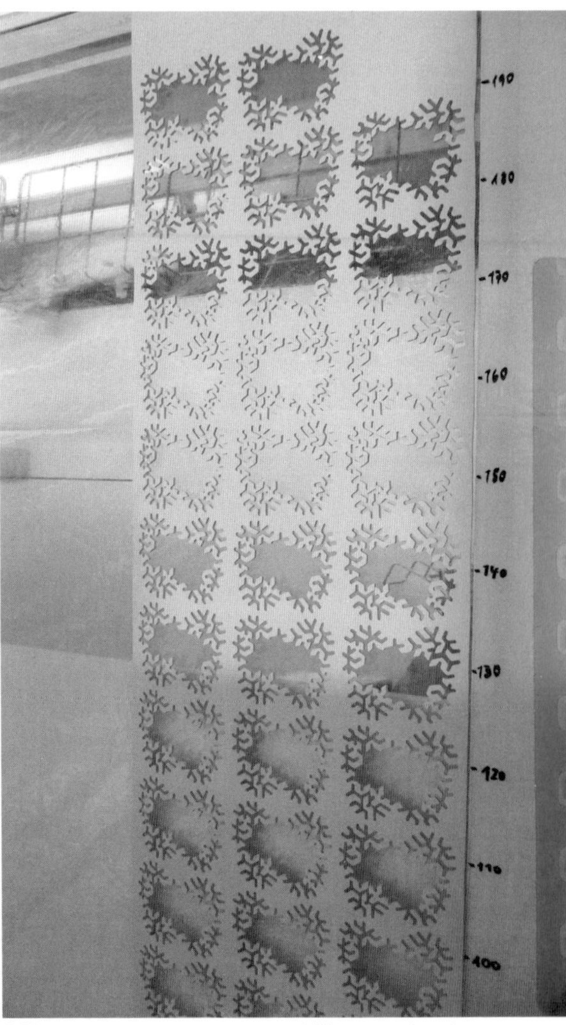

Off-cuts, computer-generated Rhizome drawings

It takes time for rhizomatic structures to occur. The computer has become a useful tool
to draw and distort, to alter, clone and mutate, to emulate growth and allow chance to
enter the creative process. The use of industrial production processes, like water-jet and
laser-technology, has opened up new possibilities and creative options.

RH—03.07—XL[112-121]

[RH−4] Rhizome wrist-piece, 2006. Natural rubber

[RH–5] **Informed Shadows**, exhibition with Anneli Tammik, 2006.
Museum of Applied Arts and Design, Tallinn, Estonia

[RH–6] Ery wearing **Rhizome**, Detroit, 2006

[RH–7] Mo wearing **Rhizome**, Llançà, 2006

[RH–8] Katie wearing **Rhizome** neckpiece, 2006. Natural rubber ├──

[RH-8]

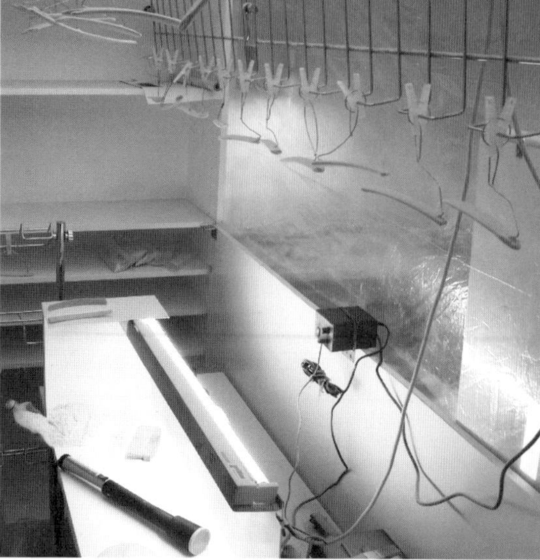

Studio views

Flocked cat and dog

OR−05.07−XL[122-133]

Ossarium Rosé

Ossarium Rosé fuses a reference to death with an unexpected sensuality suggested by soft textures and an omnipresent pink colour. The natural shapes of some bones appear as if they had been altered in order to be transformed into new ones with an imaginary function. Questions arise concerning the tension between original and fake, natural and man-made, constructed and grown. As in the *Foreign Bodies* work in medical steel (see p.94), every piece tells about the estrangement and fragility of the contemporary individual.

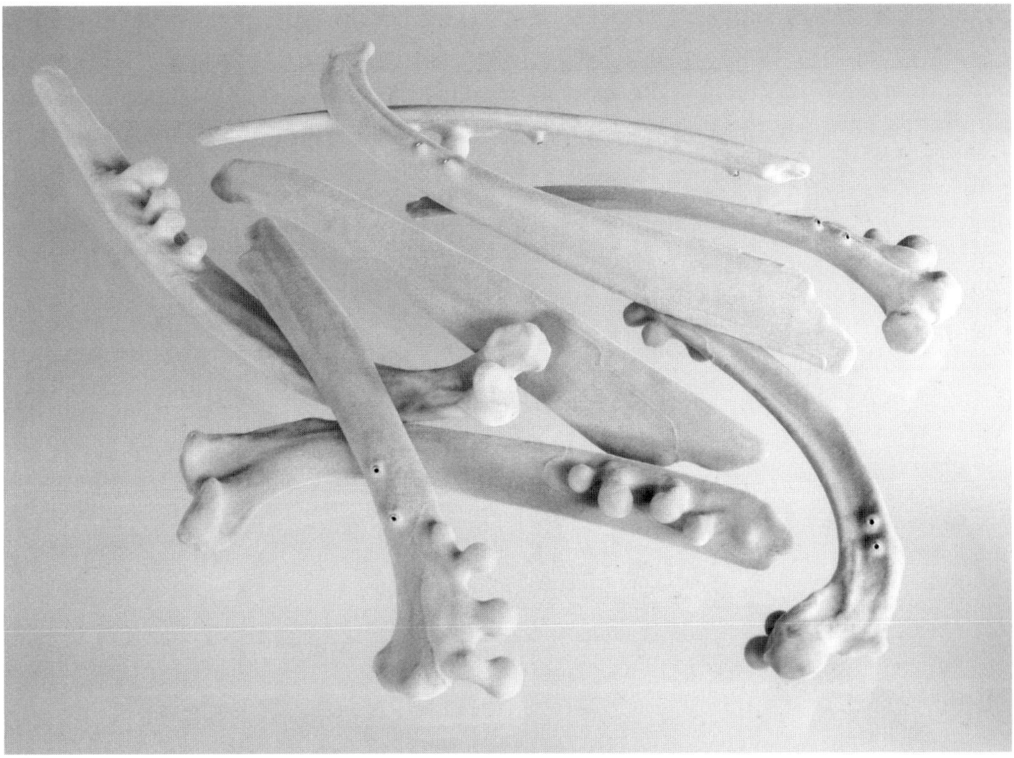

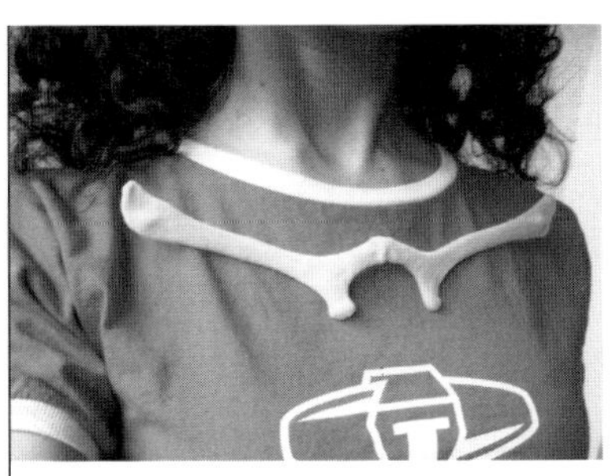

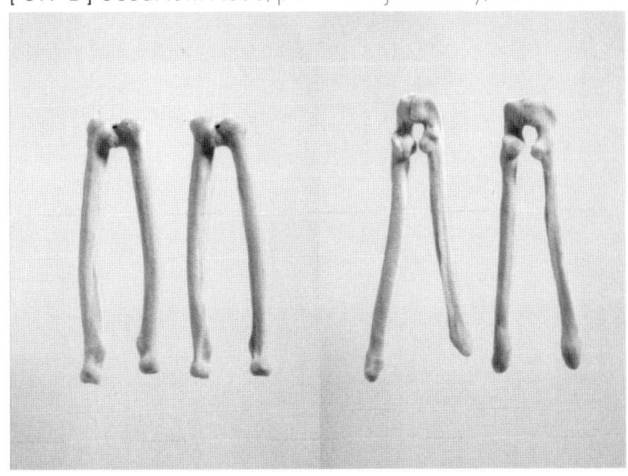

[OR–1] Ossarium Rosé, potential jewellery, 2005

"The *Relic Rosé* collection activates an emotional attachment: the worn object replaces ties with the beloved , whether living or deceased. The artist refers to the need to preserve things that serve the function of 'contemporary relics'. The works are conceived as reminders of a body that is ever more transformed, mutated and mutating." MARIA·CRISTINA BERGESIO, 2006

OR–05.07–XL[122-133]   Relic Rosé

[OR–2] Relic Rosé, 2006. Mixed media, flock, silver

[OR-2]

[OR-3] ●

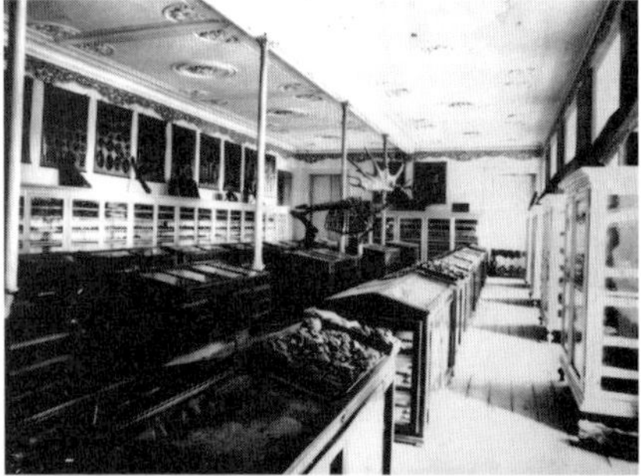

View of the original **Sala do Veado** room, named after the pre-historic deer skeleton it used to exhibit

The *Ossarium Rosé* installation in Lisbon deals with a mediated view on nature. Displayed under a cold light and orderly classified inside the only remaining showcase that survived a fire which destroyed the museum in 1978, the more than one hundred pieces acquire scientific credibility, the solemnity of the relic or the fascination of a wonder-cabinet.

OR—05.07—XL[122-133]   *Ossarium Rosé*, Lisbon, 2005

[OR—3] Relic Rosé, 2006. Mixed media, flock, silver. Private Collection

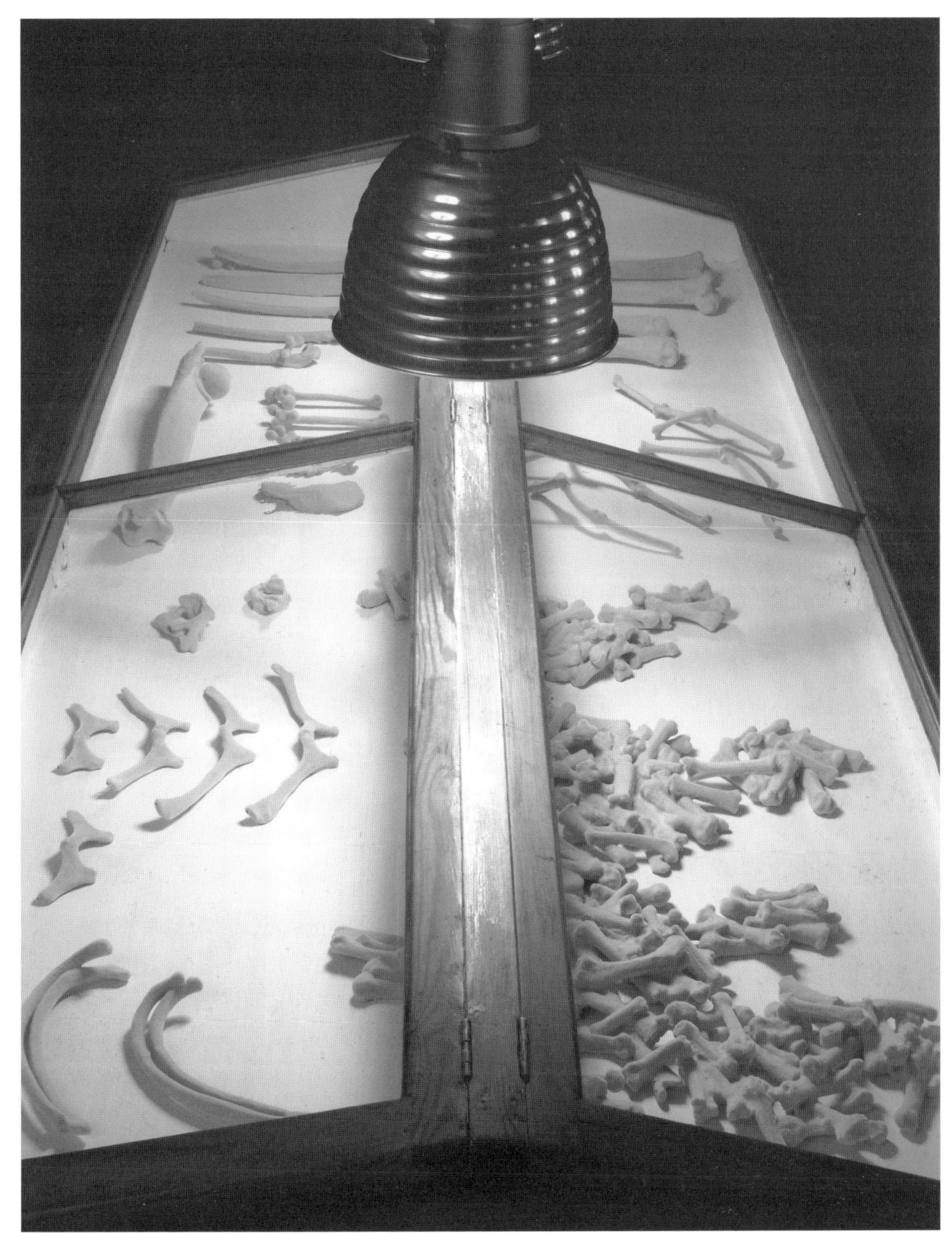

[OR–4] **Ossarium Rosé** Installation at the National Museum of Natural History, Lisbon, 2005

[OR-6] Installation **Art & Orthopædics** at the Villa de Bondt, Gent, 2006

Art & Orthopædics plays with the potentiality of objects to become jewellery. The disturbing niceness of the velvety surface that covers these bone-like objects mimics the morbidity of flesh or skin. Contradictory feelings of attraction and rejection and the distance/closeness to the body was expressed as installation and as wearable work in the domestic space of an Art Deco villa.

OR−05.07−XL[122-133]   *Art & Orthopædics*, Gent, 2006

[OR-5] Relic Rosé neckpiece, 2006. Mixed media flocked, silver

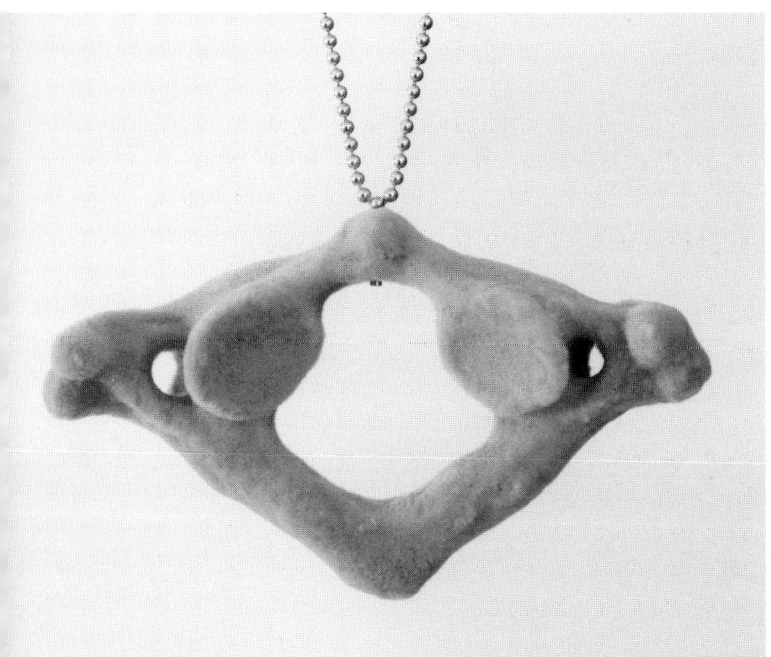

[OR-7] Relic Rosé pendant, 2006. Mixed media, flock, silver

[OR-8] Ossarium Rosé,
potential jewellery, 2005

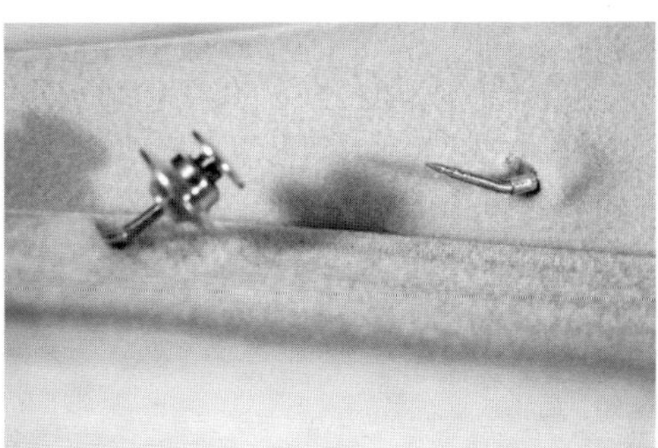

[OR-9] Relic Rosé brooches, 2006. Mixed media, flock, silver (details)

[OR-10] Art & Orthopaedics installation at the Villa de Bondt, Gent, 2006.

[OR-10]

[OR-11]

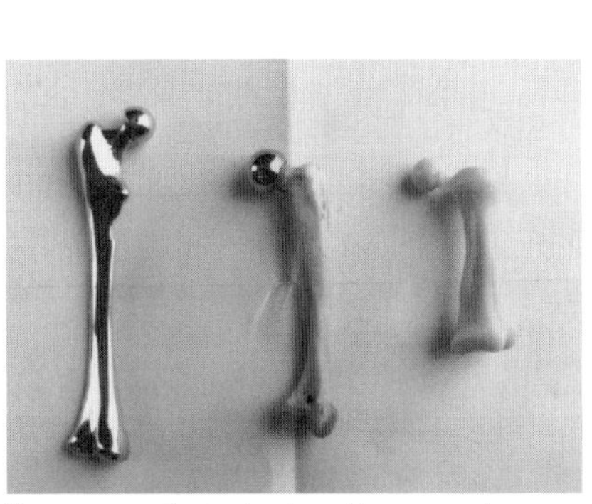

Bones, medical steel and tagua nut

Ecuador, 2006. Mercedes from the Pro Pueblo Foundation in San Antonio, Ecuador, shows a bone of her father that she preciously stores in a matchbox. This bone is the only remains she has of him after his grave was washed away during an El Niño-related flood

Tagua Works

The *Tagua* is an extremely hard nut that comes from the Ivory nut palm. It can be carved and polished like ivory making it a botanical alternative to elephant ivory or bone.

[OR-11] Relic Rosé pendant, 2006. Mixed media, flock, silver

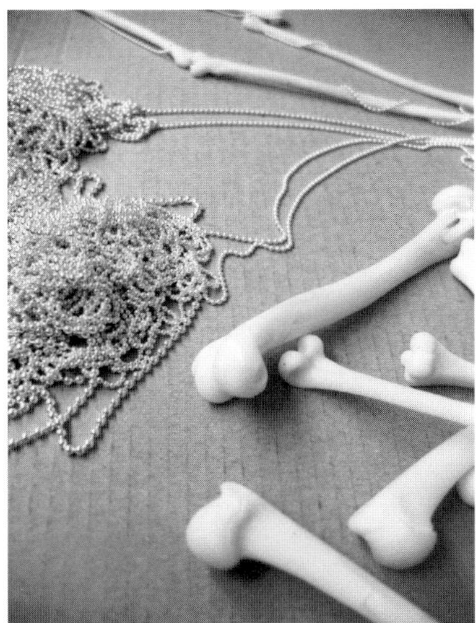

Tagua nut in different stages: natural, fried, half and fully polished, carved bones

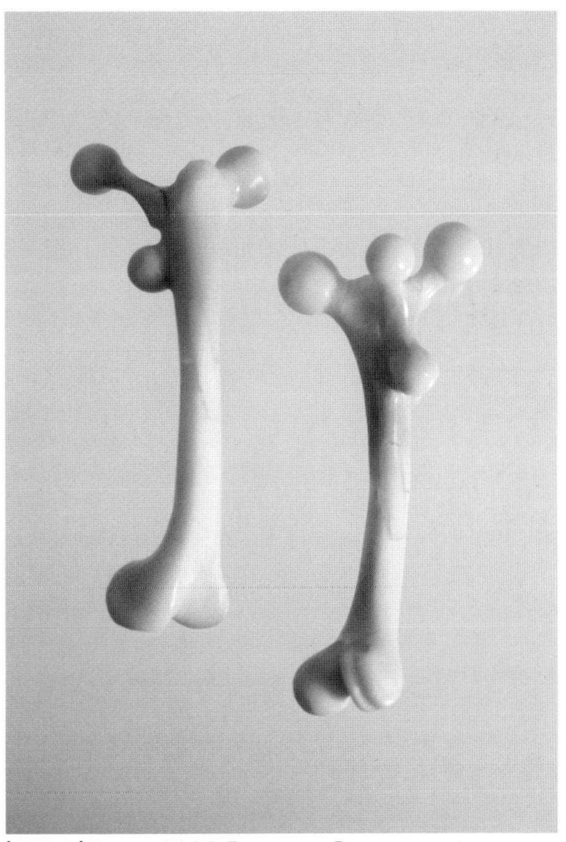

[TW–1] **Bones**, 2006. Tagua nut. Reconstruction of bone-like shapes out of several tagua pieces

"No object ever touched me more than looking at a naked bone."
CZ, 2002

[TW–2] **Bones**, 2006. Tagua nut

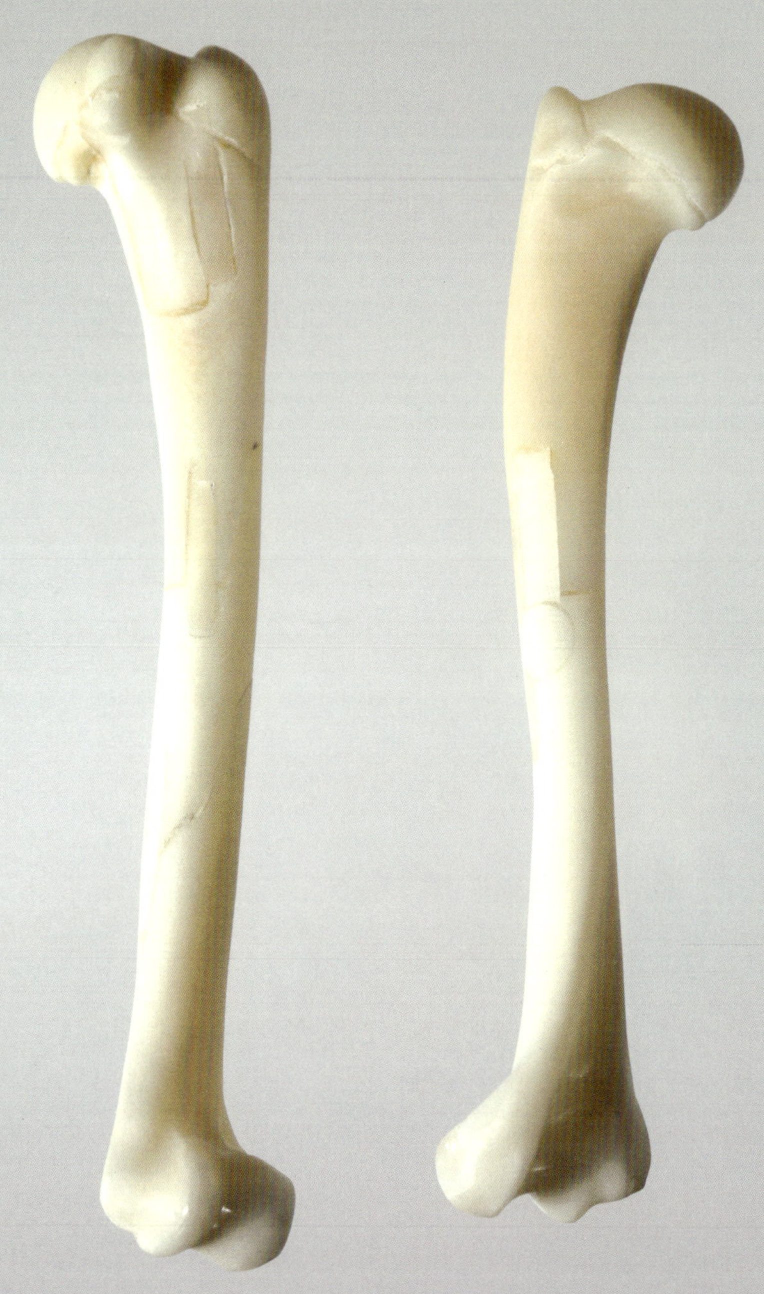

[TW-2]

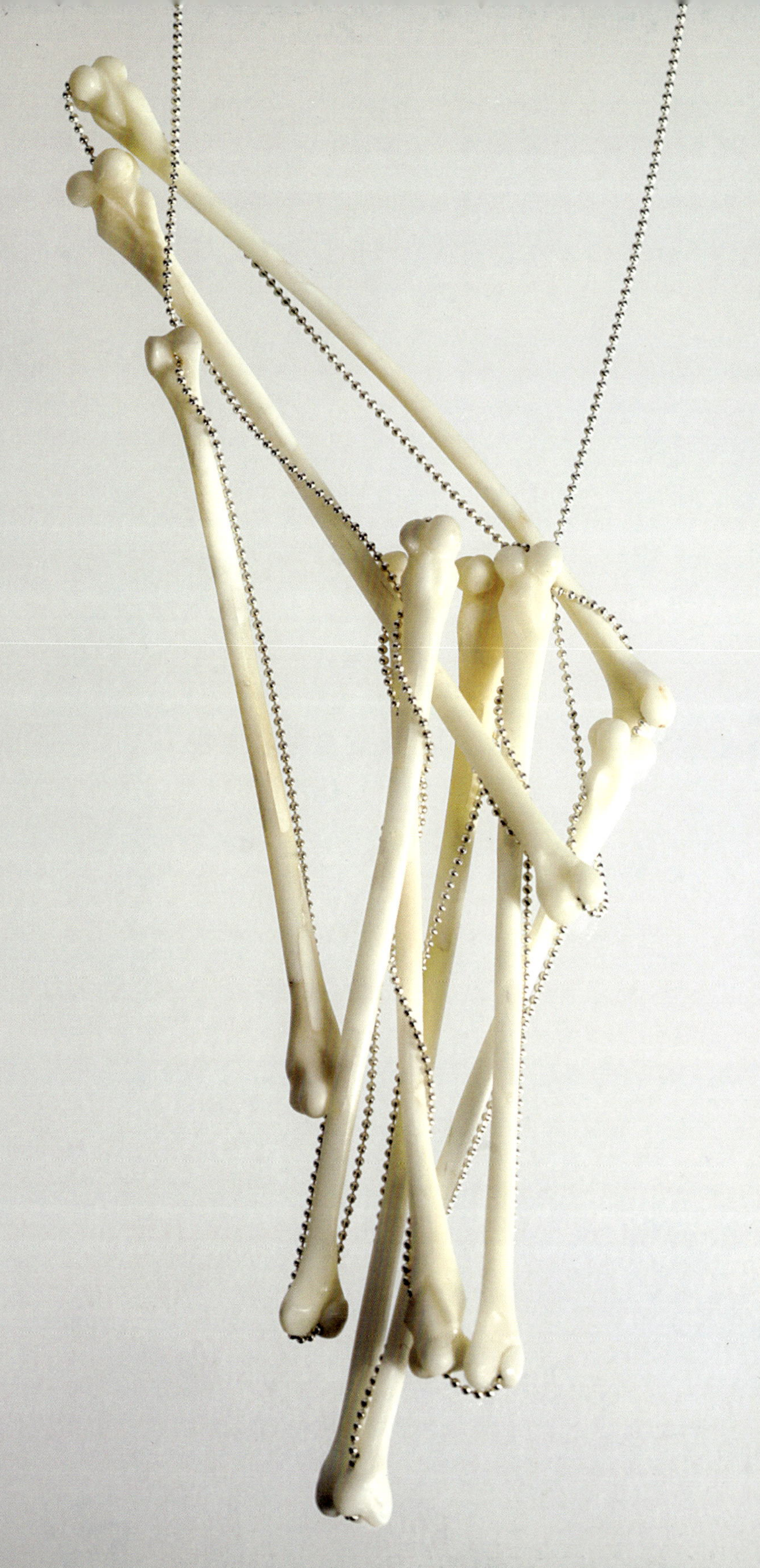

[TW-3]

THE MORNING TALK. Damian O'Sullivan, Emma Woffenden and Christoph Zellweger first met while studying in London at the Royal College of Art. After their graduation they kept in touch, kept meeting, exhibiting and talking about what mattered to them. On 6th September they arranged to meet in the new Lloyd 'Design Hotel', a setting built at the rim of Art as well as of Design, to talk about their practice. The critics Liesbeth den Besten and Mònica Gaspar took part in the dialogue and recorded the meeting. The discussion was formatted, to become one long sentence, touching upon the many issues that were talked about that Wednesday morning.

Starting with a discussion about the difference in their practice, a product designer that makes work for use and contemplation (DAMIAN), a trained glass artist doing installations (EMMA), and a traditionally trained maker/ designer of jewellery working at the rim of art and design practice (CHRISTOPH) talk about the pro's and con's of specialisation or non-specialisation. They talk about the need for **blurring categories** or staying in just one (CHRISTOPH); about understanding **design as an opportunity** for doing lots of different things (DAMIAN); about a new way of understanding the profession of making objects (MÒNICA); about wanting to make products that encourage **social change** (DAMIAN); about having a critical attitude; about having an eye on the real world and **sensing what's in the air**; about being in time, sometimes without knowing if one is really there; about the difficulty to ask colleagues to comment on ones work; about having reached a grade of professionalism that makes it impossible to get feedback; about the challenge to open oneself up; about people worrying too much about plagiarism, "copyright paranoia stops creativity" (DAMIAN), **"it may be fragile but I'm going to expose it"** (EMMA); about letting these ideas go; about the amount of time you spend to develop and **fine-tune an idea**; about the density of an idea which has to do with time" (CHRISTOPH); about trying to reveal something (EMMA); about work not needing to be analysed; about **"how to start?"**; about tracing a mental territory that suddenly materialises into something else; about wanting to leave luggage behind and therefore making a book; about already being much further (CHRISTOPH); about the good things that come from doubts; about the fact that there is **no certainty** because you are re-formatting yourself constantly; about the few good reasons for doing things; about the **small changes that matter,** about having a broad range of personalities (DAMIAN); about having the possibility 'to shift your head a bit'; about doing different things at the same time, but not being very good in **making choices** (DAMIAN); about how choices are made for you (CHRISTOPH); about what happens in the workshop being busy with one thing but picking up another; that this is the essence, "what drives me and keeps me there" (EMMA); about knowing what drives you and to make use of it; about having different nationalities or living in **different countries and cultures**; *about Damian being Irish and French living in Holland with a Dutch designer and their child who will go to a Dutch school; about Emma being British living in France with her husband who is half Dutch and*

LT–06–T[138-143]

Lloyd Talks

Ways of doing in contemporary (applied) art and design

A conversation between Emma Woffenden, Damian O'Sullivan, Iris Eichenberg, Ted Noten and Christoph Zellweger. Lloyd Hotel, Amsterdam, 6th September 2006. Transcribed and commented by Liesbeth den Besten and Mònica Gaspar

[TW–3] Bones neckpiece, 2006. Tagua nut, silver

alf Norwegian and their English born child that is now going to a French primary school; about Christoph being Swiss, with Austrian grandparents, growing up in Germany and living in England; about being back in Switzerland and living with a multi-lingual Spanish/Catalan woman, — this means nine different nationalities coming together in three people, nine different languages, nine different cultures or even more? (LIESBETH), about not identifying oneself as "national", just feeling that **"I am my own territory"**(CHRISTOPH); about the impossibility to find a truly Dutch, Swiss or British design approach in **a connected world**; about the utopia of the universal and a pre-concept that design should last forever; about the **closeness**, the discovery that design is more about the local, the working processes and sensitivity in relationship with a community (MÒNICA); about making work that should **touch people** – a piece, an installation, a product, whatever; about understanding in that very moment that one's motivation is to **create a response** (CHRISTOPH); about this meeting being like setting up a work in the studio and "looking for the invisible thing that is going to arrive" (EMMA); about **finding reason**; about making poetic porcelain prostheses as an independent designer and at the same time porcelain speakers while working in a team for *Philips*; about living in the **paradox of mass-customisation** (DAMIAN); about a social concern, about industry which will change, will have to change, in a time when things inevitably upset dramatically because of shortage of energy and oil (DAMIAN); about the attraction for the individually made, the customised, the **one offs**; about objects dense in content but so difficult to judge; about objects being nothing in the wrong context like brands without advertising; about "**object integrity**"; about the ephemeral and the sublime that resist consumption (CHRISTOPH); about putting the **emphasis on an experience**, as "nothing can have such a strong impact" (EMMA); about that story Christoph told: after an exhibition opening where he showed his work in white polystyrene, a collector of his left the gallery obviously disappointed as that work was of no **value** to her, — that the same woman came back to the gallery first thing the next morning telling the gallerist that these fragile pieces were on her mind all night and that she will never be able to look at polystyrene packaging again without **recognising beauty**, about value "created in the mind" (CHRISTOPH), — and in the guts (MÒNICA); about the different roles of art and of design, about the shift (MÒNICA); about the role of industry, about getting trapped in commerce; about the importance of designers developing work **by hand** (LIESBETH), about industry not accommodating designers to make models and to experiment directly with material (DAMIAN); about that short sightedness and that designers have again an interest in crafts (LIESBETH); about realising that budgets for education need to be **more generous** (DAMIAN AND CHRISTOPH) — everywhere; about the need for **high-tech** equipment in the college workshops, in order to see students creating imagery and using technology of their time (CHRISTOPH); — "if you **create a view** it will come back" (DAMIAN); and then after some hours the conversation ends abruptly because the tape stops and there is no time left for Emma who has to catch a train to Paris.

Emma Woffenden, Damian O'Sullivan and Christoph Zellweger
during the morning discussion

[OR-4]

THE AFTERNOON TALK

CHRISTOPH ZELLWEGER, CZ We have been working in the field of contemporary jewellery for many years, we have exhibited together, fought for new grounds and defined our own aesthetics. We have been very aware of each others development, sometimes wondered where the other is heading to, sometimes we agreed or questioned or just kept being curious in the belief, that this guy, this woman will do well and that she/he has something interesting to say…

IRIS EICHENBERG, IE Do we meet to raise questions or shall we try to find answers?

CZ Let's see where we go! How did we start? What was, what has been motivating us then, what now?

TED NOTEN, TN When I finished the Rietveld Academy my target was to have a solo show in one of those prestigious galleries.

CZ Did you manage?

TN After ten years.

IE Students today are not that interested in galleries anymore… They stop complaining about how galleries work and organize themselves, they create new platforms.

TN They team work, we were solo.

CZ That's good, they fuse. I never had the feeling that I wanted to show only in galleries. I wanted to make my things and just show them- wherever. But of course, I found out that it is good to be in the right place to reach people, and this can be a gallery.

TN …and we thought jewellery could have the same impact as the fine arts. There was a kind of competition.

CZ I think I was always going for content but not for competition. I thought the work would need to speak for itself and people would decide if they wanted to call it art.

TN I was focused on content too, but I was also looking at the art market and artistic strategies, thinking that through the way we worked jewellery might become accepted in the art world.

IE Christoph, would your work ever exist without an audience?

CZ No, but initially I don't think much in audiences. First I want to develop the idea, not in a straightforward way, but I want to say something. The work is just a vehicle for this. While I'm making I may start to think about the audience. How can the work have an impact? Will it be best to make an installation in a public space? Will it work best in a gallery?

TN My Mercedes Benz brooches started living when the audience took part in the event.

IE This is your talent to connect with people!

TN I thought my Mercedes project and the "Chew your own brooch" event would attract a new, wider audience.

IE If I do a series of works, I sometimes feel as if I plagiarize my own work. You need the distance over years to see how work is actually a repetition of storytelling. I thought everybody would read my work in the same way but I never reached the people I thought would be interested in it.

CZ What kind of people where you thinking about?

IE I thought that if I was working with body concerns, that people in the medical sector would be interested.. But people who actually had nothing to do with my subjects where the ones who could appreciate the abstraction and the poetry.

CZ Like telling something from yourself?

IE Before storytelling was a bad thing; but we are in a new period in jewellery and in fine art, they develop in the same surroundings.

TN For me there is a huge gap of how fine art and contemporary jewellery is seen.

IE I'm really allergic to the discussion about our visibility. Other experimental disciplines, like contemporary music or dance often end up not recognised enough. For me we have had this discussion too often.

CZ When there is a small audience and therefore just a small market one has to go out and create a scene. I have made a move away from galleries because I felt my work needed a different context.

TN And because you like the challenge!

CZ Because I have to create the space which works for me!

IE Everybody looks for resistance somewhere.

TN Christoph, I think you look for resistance in the process of making too. Remember how you were fighting with this polystyrene stuff!

CZ This was a fantastic process! I learned a lot about the ephemeral. I worked until certain problems disappeared also conceptually.

IE I don't know many people who spend so much time to develop a new technological process and the content in parallel. For example, the work in medical cast steel… Your mentality was always that of a scientist, I don't see often that science and art do relate that much.

CZ I am just interested in what I don't know, the unexpected. So I chose a technology that at the beginning I could not control and at the end of a long process I come up with an image, a reading of the things I make, that surprises me. When this happens I know that it will probably surprise other as well.

N You enjoy difficult processes,
ou need this delay to shape your
ontent. I am the contrary, I have an
idea and go for it.
 We are a funny tripod. I'm not a
echnician and I never work with
ideas like you do. I always try to
vercome the aesthetics of a
material. I always try to find the
order where the seductive and the
epulsive comes together and in
hat sense I try to discover my own
oncept of beauty.
N Your last series, the white one,
'as very aesthetic.
: Probably the most aesthetic
eries so far.
N I work in a different way. I make
hings and sometimes, years later,
continue with the same theme but
n different materials.
: That is what I am trying to say,
ou re-write your story but you
lways shift the content slightly.
Z So do you stay contemporary
his way?
: Well you have been making con-
emporary work for nearly twenty
ears and now you mark a moment
vith this book.
Z I'm looking for summing up
hings, putting things aside. I feel
appy with three or four subjects I
ackled but I need to move on...
N Do you want to make space?
Z I want to clean up and also put
n the book what happened in these
ears. There are new people coming
nd I'm very interested, so I like to
dentify a period.
E When we first started exhibiting
ogether someone called us "the
oung dogs" (everyone smiles) and
ometimes I wonder if once in your

life you are a "young dog" and all of
a sudden you could find yourself
being "an old sock". What happens
in between?
TN I don't find myself being an old
sock! (laughs). When you started,
what was contemporary for you?
CZ For me objects that I could not
identify immediately as jewellery but I found strong. That was
around 1984. I was a trained 'gold-
worker', you know, so I got totally
interested in what goes beyond
crafts.
IE The generation before us was
challenging values. I think we
brought in another content and a
new sensitivity. We are now in an
age of no taboos in the choice of
material, subject or whatever. But
how to deal with this freedom? If
there are no boundaries, there is
nothing to push.
TN Today most of what I see in
contemporary jewellery galleries
has the same proportions, the same
tactility, ... I get very bored.
CZ This is not new. When we
started we also found a lot of
the same. We had to overcome
the "Herman Jünger's", who were
dominating the aesthetic frame
in for a long time. There was also
the ethical polemic around the use
of gold as a statement, a public
discussion between Robert Smit
and Gijs Bakker. Pierre Degen or
Caroline Broadhead were propos-
ing the body as a stage, doing huge
objects to wear and using them in
performances.
IE They were discovering new ter-
ritories for jewellery...
CZ We tried to move on from there!

IE We could claim that we intro-
duced the anaesthetical and the
organic movement in jewellery.
CZ Karl, you, Ruudt ...
IE And today there are loads of
people making very organic work.
TN Too much!
CZ I think, Ted, that you are following a different path in the discussion about value. You make big
statements, big steps, nobody does
this like you. I think you follow on
from Manfred Nisslmüller.
TN You think so?
CZ That's what I mean with the
discussion about the contemporary. We can not exactly say what is
next, but I'm curious.
IE I do think that we can say
something about the present:
the absence of restrictions, for
example, and even the return of the
dusty word "crafts".
CZ Now many young artists and
actually designers too, deal with
ornament and decoration without
the prejudice of being considered
banal. They definitively overcame
the long shadow of Modernism. We
struggled with it...
IE When I was working on my series
of car mirrors I was reflecting on
ornament. When does something
become a pattern?
TN When I hear you talk about your
work, I think this is all so intellectual. For me the more unconscious
I am, the better works I make.
IE You should not underestimate
how close your hands are connected to your mind!
CZ The more conscious I become,
the more I refine the outcome.
For good or for bad.

Ted Noten, Iris Eichenberg and Christoph Zellweger at the end of the day

[RH-8]

CHRISTOPH ZELLWEGER
(1962, Lübeck) Swiss National

1991–1993 Royal College of Art, London, England. Master of Arts, distinction.
1987–1991 Kunstgewerbeschule, Zürich, Switzerland. Attended evening classes in sculpture.
1980–1984 Apprenticeship Goldsmith in Kiel and Lübeck, Germany.

Occupations – as maker/artist/designer
since 2003 Set up of studio/workshop *nix international*, industrial quarter, Zürich, CH
2003 designer/artist in Residence, Jakob Schlaepfer, haute-couture textiles, Sankt Gallen, CH
2001 Artist in Residence, EKWC European Ceramic Work Centre, Hertogenbosch, NL
1998–2001 Freelance designer for new technology-led venture company, Scintillate Ltd, London, UK
1993–2002 Set up of workshop in Sheffield, after 2001 at Yorkshire Art Space, UK
1984–1989 Works for several Swiss companies as modelmaker/ designer/ head of atelier, in Geneva, Lenzburg and Zürich, CH

Occupations–as educator
since 2003 Appointed Professor of Art & Design, Research, Sheffield Hallam University, Sheffield, UK
- Associated Lecturer, Industrial Design, ZHdK University of the Arts, Zürich, CH
2004–2005 Guest Professorship, Academy of Fine Arts, Nürnberg, D
1998–2002 Course Leader, MA Metalwork & Jewellery, Sheffield Hallam University, Sheffield, UK
1993–1998 Senior Lecturer, BA Hons Metalwork & Jewellery, Sheffield Hallam University, Sheffield, UK

Selected personal exhibitions and installations
2007 *Relic Rosé*, personal exhibition, Galerie Louise Smit, Amsterdam, NL [CAT]
2006 *Medical Grade 316*, intervention, Millenium Gallery, Sheffield, UK
- *Informed Shadows. Christoph Zellweger / Anneli Tammik*, Museum of Applied Arts and Design, Tallinn, EST
- *Art & Orthopædics*, personal exhibition, Galerie Villa de Bondt, Gent, B

2005 *Ossarium Rosé*, personal exhibition, National Museum of Natural History, Lisbon, P
- *Foreign Bodies*, intervention, Swiss National Museum, Zürich, CH
2004 *Knochenarbeit*, site specific installations Pro FUGE project *Kunst in Zeiten des Übergangs*, Zürich, CH
2003 *Foreign Bodies*, personal exhibition, Galerie Tactile, Geneva, CH
2001 *Pulled*, exhibition and performance, EKWC European Ceramic Work Centre, Hertogenbosch, NL
2000 *Body Pieces*, personal exhibition, Hnoss Gallery, Gothenburg, S
- *Homo Ipsi Faber*, interactive installation for *Betwixt 2*. Annual Conference of the Design History Society, Portsmouth, UK
1999 *Facts, Fakes & Beauty*, personal exhibition, Galerie Louise Smit, Amsterdam, NL [CAT]
- *Fire over Water*, outdoor performance, *Jewellery maker / Shaman?*, Gerrit Rietveld Academy, Amsterdam, NL
1998 *Christoph Zellweger*, personal exhibition, ArCo Centro de Arte e Comunicação Visual, Lisbon, P
1997 *Objects and Commodities*, personal exhibition, Galerie Schmuck Forum, Zürich, CH
1996 *Christoph Zellweger / Onno Boekhoudt*, Galerie Hélène Porée, Paris, F
1995 *Material I*, personal exhibition, Galerie für Schmuck, Zug, CH
1994 *Christoph Zellweger / Sigfried de Bück*, Gallery van Krimpen, Amsterdam, NL
1993 *Kunst auf Zeit*, Billboard installation, Prize by the Kulturamt Graz, Graz, A
1990 *Christoph Zellweger*, personal exhibition, Galerie Off Limits, Zürich, CH

Selected group exhibitions
2006 *No Body Decoration. Research Jewellery as a redefinition of the human body*, Villa Bottini, Lucca, I [CAT]
2005 *Design Labor*, Gewerbemuseum, Winterthur, CH. (Traveling to Kornhausforum, Bern, 2006) [CAT]
- *Nomad Room. Contemporary Jewellery, Intimate Space and Public Domain*, CCB Design Museum, Lisbon, P [CAT]
- *What's Luxury?* Chi a Paura...? Foundation, Salone del Mobile, Milano, I
2004 *Body Extensions*, MUDAC Musée de Design et d'Arts Appliqués Contemporains, Lausanne, CH
- *Meeting Point(s)*, Centro de Arte Moderna José de Azeredo Perdigão, Lisbon, P [CAT]

2003 *Corporal Identity. Body Language. 9th Triennial for Form & Content*, MAK Museum for the Applied Arts Frankfurt, D. (Traveling to Museum of Art & Design, New York) [CAT]
- *Luxe Interior. Inner Luxury. International Contemporary Jewellery*, CaixaForum, Year of Design, Barcelona, E [CAT]
- *Crafts Now. 21 Artists from America, Europe and Asia*, Kanazawa World Craft Forum, Kanazawa, Japan [CAT]
- *Art Jewellery in Switzerland in the 20th Century*, Musée d'Art et d'Histoire, Geneva, CH (Traveling to Museo Vela, Ligornetto and Schweizerisches Landesmuseum, Zürich) [CAT]
2002 *Trois Visions d'un Corps. Sophie Hanagart, Paul Mc Clure, Christoph Zellweger*, Espace Solidor, Cagnes sur Mer, F [CAT]
- *Capolavori: l'artista artigiano tra Picasso e Sottsass*, Palazzo Bricherasio, Turin, I [CAT]
- *Slip. Artists in the Netherlands and Britain working with ceramics*, Frans Hals Museum, Haarlem, NL. (Traveling to Sainsbury Centre, Norwich, UK) [CAT]
2001 *The Breath of Nature. International Craft Biennale 2001*, Cheongju City, South Korea [CAT]
- *Mikromegas*, BKV, Münich, D. (Traveling to American Craft Museum, New York; Gallerie YU, Tokyo; Powerhouse Museum, Sydney) [CAT]
- *Waldeslust. Iris Eichenberg, Hilde de Decker, Christoph Zellweger*. Gallerie V&V, Vienna, A
2000 *Design Mensch*, Museum für Kunst und Gewerbe, Hamburg, D
- *Kunst hautnah–Virtuelles, Visuelles, Haptisches*, Künstlerhaus Wien, Vienna, A [CAT]
- *Alles Schmuck. Collection Asenbaum*, Museum für Gestaltung, Zürich, CH [CAT]
- *The Ego Adorned, 20th Cent Art Jewellery*, Queen Fabiola Hall, Antwerp, B [CAT]
- *Jerwood Prize 2000*, finalist, travelling exhibition, The Crafts Council, London, UK [CAT]
1998 *European Prize for Contemporary Art & Design-led Crafts*, WCC, Viena, A; Gothenburg, S; Paris, F [CAT]
1996 *Objects of Our Time*. The Crafts Council, London, UK [CAT]
- *New Times New Thinking. Jewellery in Europe & America*, The Crafts Council, London, UK [CAT]
1994 *Works for '94*, Crafts Council Gallery, London, UK [CAT]

[RH–8] "Thinking of you, of rhizomes, non-hierarchical systems, states and patterns..."

Awards

Prize of the Communauté Française de Belgium, B

Swiss Federal Prize for Design, 2002/1998/1995, Kulturamt Bern, CH

D&AD, British Design & Art Direction, membership award, UK

Shortlisted Jerwood Prize, London, UK

Herbert Hofmann Prize–International Award, Munich, D

Prize by the Kulturamt Graz, Outdoor Installation in the City of Graz, A

Individual Artists Award, Yorkshire and Humberside Arts, UK

Robinson Charitable Trust Award, London, UK

Public Collections

Museum für Angewandte Kunst, Frankfurt, D

Swiss National Museum, Zürich, CH

Schmuckmuseum Pforzheim, D

Contemporary Arts Society, UK

Musee d' Horlogerie, Geneva, CH

Museum für Kunst und Gewerbe, Hamburg, D

MIMA. Institute of Modern Art, Middlesborough, UK

ArCo Permanent Collection of Art, Lisbon, P

National Foundation for Contemporary Art–FNAC, Paris, F

British Crafts Council, London, UK

Royal Mint Collection, London, UK

Angermuseum, Erfurt, D

Masterclasses / Educational projects (selected)

2006/07 Cranbrook Academy of Art, Detroit, Michigan, USA

2005/06/07 *Pro Pueblo Design*, project in Zürich–Ecuador, HGKZ University of Applied Sciences and Arts, Zürich, CH

2005 *The Perfect Flow*, ESAD School of Art and Design, Porto, P; ARCO, Lisbon

Jewellery Design in Context, professor, International Summer Academy Salzburg, A

2004/05/06 *No Risk No Gain*, Adellab, Konstfack University of Art & Design, Stockholm, S

2004/05 Projects, University College of Art and Design, Loughborough, UK

2001/02 *Material & Technology*, Haute École d'Artes Appliques, Geneva, CH

2000 Project, HDK School of Design and Crafts, Gothenburg, S

1999 *Interface Skin*, Design Werkstatt, International Summer School, Braunwald, CH

- *Interface Skin*, Karl de Grote Hogeschool, Antwerp, B

1997 Jewellery workshop, Onno Boekhoudt and Christoph Zellweger, International Summer School, Jazzenuil, F

1995/99/01 Projects, Gerrit Rietveld Academy, Amsterdam, NL

1992/98/04/05 *Enhancing Jewellery and Mr Vacanti; 30 Hours*, Ar.Co Centro de Arte I Comunicação Visual, Lisbon, P

Lectures (selected)

2006 Cranbrook Academy of Art, Detroit Michigan, USA

- *Art & Orthopedics*, Orthopædica Belgica Congress, Gent, B

2004 *Foreign Bodies*, Ar.Co Centro de Arte I Comunicação Visual, Lisbon, P

2003 *Homo Sapiens, ein Auslaufmodell?* for Körper/Kunst, Museum of Applied Art, Frankfurt, D

2002 *Out of the pressure cooker, into the Firewire*, at Conference, *Pixel Raiders, Applied Artists and Digital Technologies*, Victoria & Albert Museum, London, UK

2001 *Facts, Fakes and Beauty*, Bauhaus Archive, Berlin, D

1996 *Homo Ipsi Faber*, for *Savage Luxury?*, Business and Design Centre, London, UK

Talks / Lectures (selected) at: Central Saint Martins College of Art and Design, London; Royal College of Art, London; Middlesex University, London; Coventry School of Art and Design, Coventry; Buckinghamshire Chilterns Uni College, High Wycombe, UK; Parlament Lyceen Europeen, Arezzo, I; The Diamond Museum, Antwerp, B; South Carelia Politechnic, Lappenranta, FIN; Zimmerhof–Haldenhof Symposiums, D; HKB Hochschule der Künste, Bern, CH …

Selected bibliography

Books

- REIJNDERS, Anton, **The Ceramic Process. European Ceramic Work Centre.** Philadelphia: University of Pennsylvania Press / London: A & C Black, 2005.

- GRANT, Catherine (ed.), **New directions in jewellery.** London: Black Dog Publishing, 2005.

- CRIVELLI, Patrizia; MICHEL, Ralf; MÜLLER, Lars. (eds.), **Swiss Design. Netzwerke. Réseaux. Networks.** Bern: Bundesamt für Kultur, 2002.

- FABIAN, Andreas; TEN HOMPEL, Simone (eds.), **A Field of Silver.** Wolverhampton: Buckinghamshire Chilterns University Press, 2002.

- BRITISH DESIGN & ART DIRECTION, **38th Annual of the best in British and International Design and Advertising.** London: BD & AD, 2000.

- ZELLWEGER, Christoph, **Christoph Zellweger 1990–1999.** Sheffield: EgG Design, 1999.

- RIKLIN-SCHELBERT, Antoinette, **Schmuck Zeichen. 20th Century Swiss Art Jewellery.** St Gallen: VGS, 1999.

- POWERS, Alan, **Nature in Design.** London: Conran Octopus Publishing, 1999.

- FRAYLING, Christopher, **Art and Design. 100 years RCA.** London: Collins & Brown, 1999.

- LAMBERT, Sylvie. **The Ring. Past & Present.** Singapur: Rotovision, 1998.

- TAYLOR, Louise. **No Picnic.** London: The Crafts Council, 1998.

- DU CERVAL, Marguerite (ed.) **Dictionaire International Bijou.** Paris: Editions du Regard, 1998.

- TURNER, Ralph. **New Times New Thinking. Jewellery in Europe & America.** London: Thames & Hudson, 1996.

Interviews / Articles

- DEN BESTEN, Liesbeth, "Ossarium Rosé", in *Vormberichten*. Amsterdam: BNO, September, 2005.

- GLAUSER, Stefanie, "Christoph Zellweger. Schmuck Design", Zürich, May-October, 2005. (Unpublished, CZ archive).

- YALLOP, Jacqueline, "Worked to the bones" in *Ceramic Review*. nº 207. May-June. London, 2004.

- DANKOW, Karolina, "Räucherstäbchen in den Ruinen" in *Neue Zürcher Zeitung*, Zürich: 2nd March, 2004.

- MAAS, Barbara, "Was vom Körper übrig bleibt" in *Kunsthandwerk + Design*. Frechen: Ritterbach Verlag, May-June 3/2003.

- WILLIAMS, Hilary, "Pixel Raiders" in *[a-n] Magazine for Artists*, London, 2001.

- CASTRO CALDAS, Manuel, "A Jewel once you say so" in *Christoph Zellweger 1990–1999*. Sheffield: EgG Design, 1999.

www.nixinternational.eu

[FB-14]

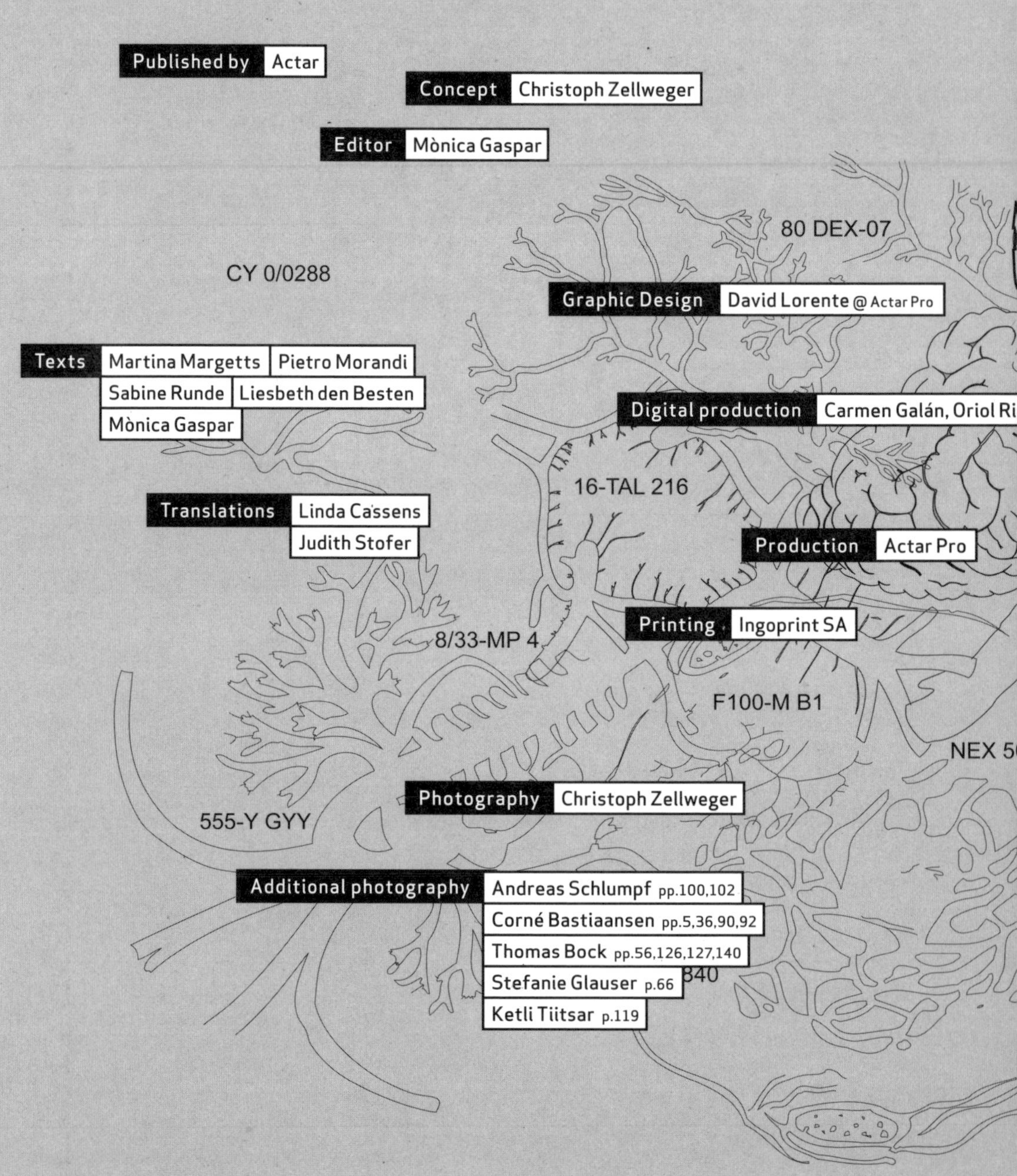

Foreign Bodies

Credits